Andrew
Give us a
Kiss

To Carrie

Best Wishes

Lawrence Gordon.
9/03/2010.

Lawrence Gordon

© Copyright 2007 Lawrence Gordon
All rights reserved. No part of this publication may be reproduced, stored in a retrieval system, or transmitted, in any form or by any means, electronic, mechanical, photocopying, recording, or otherwise, without the written prior permission of the author.

Note for Librarians: A cataloguing record for this book is available from Library and Archives Canada at www.collectionscanada.ca/amicus/index-e.html
ISBN 1-4251-1815-1

Printed in Victoria, BC, Canada. Printed on paper with minimum 30% recycled fibre. Trafford's print shop runs on "green energy" from solar, wind and other environmentally-friendly power sources.

Offices in Canada, USA, Ireland and UK

Book sales for North America and international:
Trafford Publishing, 6E–2333 Government St.,
Victoria, BC V8T 4P4 CANADA
phone 250 383 6864 (toll-free 1 888 232 4444)
fax 250 383 6804; email to orders@trafford.com
Book sales in Europe:
Trafford Publishing (UK) Limited, 9 Park End Street, 2nd Floor
Oxford, UK OX1 1HH UNITED KINGDOM
phone +44 (0)1865 722 113 (local rate 0845 230 9601)
facsimile +44 (0)1865 722 868; info.uk@trafford.com
Order online at:
trafford.com/07-0225

10 9 8 7 6 5 4 3

My own thanks:

Thanks to my wife Avril and family for giving me the time and inspiration to write this book about Andrew.

Thanks to our neighbours, and in particular to David and Anita Betts, who for years have been incredibly gracious to my family.

Thanks to all those friends and carers who have made our lives that much richer with Andrew.

CONTENTS

1) Foreword 7
2) Who am I? 9
3) Early Days: the First Year. 11
4) Challenges: for me and my parents. 19
   - Walking at last. 22
   - Food and drink. 27
   - Sight. 30
   - Touch. 32
   - Good habit, Bad habit. 33
5) More Obsessions or 'How I can really wind dad up!' 37
6) Just a normal day in the life of Andrew Miles Gordon. 44
7) Humour. 51
8) Thank you to all my Friends and Carers. 58
   - Education. 65
9) Partying. 73
10) Friends and Family. 78
11) My Mum and Dad. 96
12) Lessons we have all learned. 102

Foreword

Writing the book has been very therapeutic for me and has enabled me to see Andrew in a totally different light. For years I could not adapt to the thought of having a handicapped child, and in my own way rebelled, at times quite badly. What effect this had on Andrew, and my family, one can only guess. And this was further compounded by the fact that the cause of Andrew's medical condition has never been officially identified.

However, I have tried to write, 'Andrew Give us a Kiss' as though he, Andrew, had written it. Seeing through his eyes I wondered if, had he been able to write, he would have written like I have, but from his perspective of course. This part of the exercise I have found very hard to put into words at times, but hope for the reader, and Andrew, that I have succeeded. Sometimes Andrew is like any other normal adult: humorous, understanding, appreciative, moody, depressed, and he has loads of other traits that are quite 'normal'. All these emotions he displays without being able to speak, and the frustrations he must experience at times I can see drive him to distraction. I have also tried to recall those times when, as parents, we can remember things about our children that they forget. We also know that children remember things about their parents that the parents have long forgotten, but that impacted on their children at the time. Andrew is no different to this, in his way naturally. I know that Andrew has memories, particularly about food and drink, and of course he acknowledges faces that he has warmed to, as we all do. And so it was, that having looked Andrew long and hard in the eye, I believe he might, just might, have written something similar to this book if he could write. Although we will never know for sure, I know he has been aware of me tapping on the keyboard, especially at weekends when we share so much time together.

What I do know is that the shared experiences with Andrew, whether with family or friends, have never been at such a high level of development as they were when I was writing the book. Watching him try and perform certain tasks and rituals has been mind-blowing these last couple of years as he has absorbed his Omega 3 fish oil! But hey, that is all in the book.

His personality has continued to develop all the time and at times, he is what in our family language we call a 'Little Minx'.

I like to think Andrew would enjoy this book. After all, he wrote it.

Lawrence Gordon. November 2006.

Who am I?

Andrew Miles Gordon, 35 years old last March 21st, and the elder of two children, eldest of three if you count the dog.

Mum, Avril, and Dad, Lawrence, are both retired teachers - or they should be but they never switch off. Sister Anna, married to Mike, she's not like mum and dad at all. She's a good mate. And last but not least, Merrie, the blue roan cocker spaniel – thinks she owns the house and was obviously a teacher in a former life, and it shows.

I'm 5 foot 9 inches tall and weigh 10 stone 7 pounds, but 11 stone if Dad cooks at the weekend. My eyes are green, my hair greying – thanks Dad - and I have a nose like a ski slope after breaking it several times years ago.

I have lived all my life in Birmingham where I was born in 1972, and have travelled around most of England, most of Wales and large parts of Scotland, but I have never been abroad, and it looks like I never will.

I live with my parents in a large four bed-roomed

semi in Sutton Coldfield and I have three main hobbies: food, cars and aeroplanes. I spend a great deal of time on these hobbies which I have worked on progressively as I get older. My bedroom reflects my car and plane hobbies to a large extent, with loads of pics that Mum and Dad have bought, and I have a big collection of badges on my bedroom wall which family and friends supplement when they visit far away places.

My fashion sense is limited to 'posh casual' and if I'm honest my Mum buys most of my clothes, which she thinks I look quite dandy in.

I have no girlfriend and although I have a close friend, Keith, we only share time together at Brooklands Hospital in the West Midlands.

Oh, and by the way, I am severely brain-damaged with 'learning difficulties', have autistic tendencies, cannot speak and my Mum and Dad do everything for me, including putting these words on my paper!

So that's me, in a brief sort of way, and I hope you will stay with me as I tell you about some of my life's experiences and challenges, not without a great sense of humour, laughter and fun, but with some heartbreak too.

Early Days: the First Year.

Much of what follows in this section is difficult for me, Andrew, to comment on for reasons you will soon see. Not being there at the very beginning is a decided disadvantage, but I have heard ………………….

In 1971 my Mum, Avril, was advised to start a family by her doctor after she had minor surgery in that same year. And, by the time her contraceptive pills had hit the floor outside our bedroom window, she was pregnant. No long practice sessions here then, just Wham! Bam! I think I am! Pregnant of course and this was confirmed in the August school holidays. Needless to say another celebratory curry!

Mum's pregnancy was uneventful in that it progressed normally: visits to the doctor, and ante natal clinic for check-ups, and Mum continued teaching PE for 6 months of her pregnancy.

The birth was not easy, and was induced because Mum, or rather I, was 7-10 days late and there followed a long labour and a high forceps delivery and I appeared eventually at 9lbs 1oz, with a large haematoma each side of my head. Her womb was to invert, rather like turning an envelope inside out, and the afterbirth was still attached to it. Difficult and nasty, not very nice, but Mum and baby survived despite the inherent problems. That night the local public house took a hammering as dad's football team, and cricket team wet the baby's head. Soaked is perhaps a better description! And of course the celebratory curry followed. Eventually after several days in the Marston Green Maternity Hospital and after registering the birth, getting rid of my jaundice, we went home as a family of three for the first time and began the baby routine so familiar to all mums and dads. That is, feed, nappy change, feed, nappy change etc and a bath-time with ducks and boats and water bottles to look forward to, but didn't expect to have water fights with Mum. So it was with us, after all, at this time I was apparently the same as every other baby that Mum and Dad knew and had known.

Feeding me was not a problem: plenty of breast milk that I adored, but quirkily, I only ever suckled on one side until Mum turned me round under her arm, on her other side. Then, apart from the 'windy' smiles I apparently slept well between feeds. In the night I was quite good and apart from the night feed, went back to sleep really well, having exhausted my mother. Not that I would remember.

Between 4-6 Months mum noted my development was slow and not progressing as it should have done. So, while visiting the local clinic, Mum informed the community nurses that she suspected all was not as it should be with me. 'Slow development'; 'a lazy boy'; 'he'll develop soon' were the regular comments from those community nurses. Then the best comment of all: 'You're not stimulating him enough, Mrs Gordon'. Shit! I had more toys from Fisher-Price, in and around the lounge, than half the shops in Birmingham. You could not move without tripping over some educational toy bought by a well-meaning friend or relation.

Still, I was a Mum's boy and Mum and Dad loved me to bits, no matter what my problems. However, they had to begin seeking out specialists in child development for everyone's sake, not least mine, Andrew Gordon.

Not helping the situation, Dad somehow contracted encephalitis in July 1972, and Mum was now dealing with three problems: my development which was clearly causing her great heartache, but the possibility of her losing her husband was a double whammy, and her own mum had just had a hysterectomy. Dad recovered after several months and was again able to support Mum again with me. However, there was a problem at the doctors'. Mum and Dad did not feel that doctors and nurses were being honest with them about me and so they asked and were referred to the Child Development unit at Good Hope Hospital after Xmas 1972. I was approaching my first birthday.

First Xmas 1972

If they were hoping for a change in attitude regarding my progress, or were hoping for a lifeline in the future for me, they were very much mistaken. When they asked to be given a blunt indication of my future prospects, what the consultant paediatrician told them flattened my Mum and Dad utterly and forever.

'Andrew may never walk, talk or feed himself. He is going to need a lot of looking after for the rest of his life.'

The drive home was in silence, all 10 miles of it. Tears flowed, and do to this day, especially when there are young 'scrotes' as Dad calls them, walking around being abusive and foul. It still gets to him that I am not what they had expected me to be. So, he's still angry and screwed up after all these years – it gets you that way sometimes.

Even when still visiting the clinic, after my first birthday, some of the nurses pooh-poohed the idea that I was brain-damaged, and although they thought they were being helpful, really they were raising Mum and Dad's hopes unrealistically. My Nanny Gordon was the same, always looking for some clue that I was going to be all right and normal, because 'Doctors have been wrong before, you know,' she kept saying. Well, they weren't with me, mate, so the sooner people accepted the score the better things would be and that would mean some progress. Or not, as the case may be.

Some days were worse than others for my parents as they were adjusting to what was going to be required for me. Dad went back to teaching, but he was aware of leaving Mum at home still heartbroken over me, as they both were really, but nonetheless, Mum was at home. My pram was the Rolls-Royce of prams, purchased by my mum's adoring parents, and the hardest part of all, for my Mum and Dad, was when friends and family pushed their faces into my pram looking for signs of progress. Struggling to come to terms with my lack of progress, they knew full well that any would be so miniscule as to be immeasurable. A smile, a turn of the head, a burp, a windy break from mouth or rear or even a blink were all guaranteed to be recorded in the parental 'brain-diary' of my progress.

And still the visits to hospital or doctor proceeded at a good rate, and were probably doing more for Mum and Dad rather than me, as we all adjusted to a life they had not been expecting. One of the hardest parts in all this was to fathom out why I looked so normal, I was such a bonny baby and didn't look 'handicapped'. So why was I? Why, oh why, oh why? Why pick on Mum? Why Dad? For crying out loud, they had been so damned happy as a couple and so looking forward to having a family – Why? Why? Why?

This part of their lives should have been happy with a young baby occupying not only their time, but also their optimism and happiness for the future, but it was to proving testing to say the least. They were going through the wringer and were going to be examined, as never before, as a couple – for better or for worse.

In Gorleston with Mum

Ready for bed

It didn't occur to Dad for some time that they could call on extra help and so they had me christened at a local church where friends and family were very supportive for that lovely day. A wonderful vicar, Francis Chadwick, took the service and while he remained in the parish for a while longer, tried very hard to help Mum and Dad in coming to terms with me and my problems. Not so though his replacement who gave Dad the 'Glen Hoddle response' for my condition: that in a previous life I, Andrew, had clearly done something so horrendous that this was my punishment. On the basis that a child might read this text, I will only let on that the second word Dad used to this vicar was 'off!' Needless to say he was never allowed in our house again. Insensitive? I think he was. Particularly as a young couple were beginning to adjust to life with a handicapped child, and at that time, not very well at all. Nowadays, perhaps, parents are given more advice and coping strategies in a similar position.

The reader must not think that life for Dad and Mum was all doom and gloom at this time. Far from it. They carried on their life, sports – I'm told Dad bowled 10 miles an hour quicker on the cricket field. Mum too, for a limited time continued playing netball, and took me with her to games. But in their private times together, when the curtains closed, or when the lights were switched off last thing at night, their mind went into overdrive. Gremlins, big ones, played havoc with their thoughts but they did have their humour, laughter and fun too, as you can read later. It just so happened that this period their life was un-planned, unprepared for, and they just did not cope with what was thrown at them.

Challenges: for me and my parents.

Challenge, or to test, especially in a stimulating way, is but one definition of that word. My behaviour and development over the years has, to say the least, been challenging and I hope I am now able to illustrate some of the challenges that have confronted me and my family and friends throughout my life.

In the last chapter, I described some of the pressures that all parents face when babies are born and the learning curve that is presented to them. Not much time for practice when the real thing arrives, eh? Obviously I cannot remember much from those days, but Mum and Dad must have learned pretty fast under the circumstances I presented them with.

I suppose the first thing that Mum and Dad noticed about my progress or lack of it, was the lack of smiles or facial expressions and lack of motor development.

Somehow I was just not able to move like my friends did. My hands were OK to look at but they did not grasp Mum's breasts at feeding time, which I loved, like other breast-fed friends. So doubts were raised early on and were compounded when I would not sit up or crawl at the normal time. But that didn't stop Mum and Dad giving me a kiss for my efforts. And all the time I was getting bigger and drinking more of Mum's milk. Nothing wrong there, but boy could I fill nappies - I'd have got gold had it been an Olympic event! Solid foods did not even stimulate my appetite from the time I graduated to them. But still I was not clasping Mum's spoon with my hands like other babies.

Not sitting up like my mates began to upset Mum and Dad, but I just could not manage it as I kept falling over slowly to the side as I lost my balance. The silly nurses at the clinic said I was lazy, but they knew nothing. Dad drove Mum and I regularly to hospitals and on one occasion they cried all the way home, but no-one told me what was wrong with me. Later, I used to go back to the hospital and nurses and doctors did all sorts of things to me: sitting me up, but I fell over; prodding me, but I never seemed to respond; shining lights in my eyes which blinded me and rang bells and made noises behind screens. That last one was a good game compared with the others and I could move my head to where the noise was. Good eh?

Much, much later, after my first birthday Mum and Dad began to sit me up on my bum and with lots of concentration I could stay sitting. But then I'd fall over and wipe the smile from my parent's faces sadly. And then they'd prop me up again and the laughing and smiles returned until ... you've got it, I fell over again. But Dad would still give me a kiss, and then ask me for a kiss. Cheering me up, I suppose. The same happened when they wanted me to walk, or thought I should be walking. Mum would hold me under the arms and expect me to move my feet forward, but I didn't know how to make them move. So they would pump my legs like pistons to let me feel how it should be. But I wasn't having any of that. Not then anyhow.

But I made everyone happy when at about 14 months I began to shuffle on my bottom: Mum would put me on my bottom and leave and watch me as if I were a sea-lion, and one day, accidentally it must have been, I put my knee nearer to my tummy, and then again with the other leg, and I moved. Mum clapped and screamed and told Dad when he came from school and I had to perform all night. Of course I got hugs and kisses again, and yes, Dad asked me to give him a kiss. God, I was tired that night. Soon I was moving everywhere, forward, backwards and round in circles. I soon began to enjoy this because people came to see me perform and clapped me and picked me up, and some even kissed me – ugh! (Dad still asks me to give him a kiss to this day. I sometimes think he's pleased with me, but maybe he's found his feminine side.)

Summer 1974

Walking at last.

I had been slow to walk, as I didn't even crawl. Then one day, when I was perhaps 18 months old I shuffled over to the settee and began to pull myself up. One doctor said I would see more from this shuffling! However, I fell over right away, of course, but I kept on trying and then, I stood up. Wow, I thought. You can see much more from here. And so shuffling and pulling myself up on chair legs, or the like, let me have a new life, so to speak. But still I could not walk and that worried Mum and Dad. Even my baby walker and bouncer were of no help at this stage.

Going to the hospital didn't help either, because I just could not do what the nurses and doctors asked me to do. The look on Mum and Dad's faces told me that they were disappointed, but I just could not hold my balance. Walker machines with wheels didn't help either: I could move about but not take the weight on my legs. Reins were a waste of space too at this time, but would be useful later as I got older. Still, I kept on trying, kept falling over, kept being picked up, but never gave up hope.

When I was two and a half / three years old I had had enough practice falling over and decided to try harder, and one day it worked and I was off walking, to my surprise. Only a few steps before the inevitable, but I walked. As time passed I got better and better, walking further and walking all around the house. The only problem was if I was confronted by any uneven surface and then I went over. If the ground was uneven or undulating I had the same problem. And throughout all this time, as I was learning to walk, my little sister Anna was also beginning to crawl and walk too: she was so quick to learn, and I could not believe how quickly she developed. Women!

With my lovely sister Anna.

Throughout my life Mum and Dad have always had to take great care of me because I don't seem to be aware of danger. I would, if they let me, probably walk out into the road and get injured or worse. Sometimes, when walking, I would just sit down right there on the pavement and would not move for ages. People used to stare at me but I didn't care. Dad used to get angry and begin to tell me off, sometimes very loudly, but Mum would tell him off too, so he'd pick me up and carry me. That always worked!

People, some who should know better, used to stare at me too. An occasion that springs to mind occurred when I was just two years old, in a Tesco store. Mum and Dad, with me in the trolley, were completing the weekend shopping as two elderly ladies went past us in the aisle and commented on my shouting and screaming saying that children like me should have been 'put down at birth!' Well, just before World War Three broke out, Dad quietly, without Mum knowing, wheeled me round the store until he found the ladies again going about their business. Wheeling me quickly he 'diplomatically' approached them and told them if he heard them talk like that about me again, then they too would end up brain damaged! He then just wheeled me away, as if nothing had happened. I said he had a short fuse, my Dad, but at least he has always stuck up for me.

When I had to go into parks for a walk the same problems occurred with uneven ground or walking up a slope. I don't know why, but sometimes I could not move. I could just about walk sideways slowly and if I didn't, someone would have to come to my rescue and offer me a hand. Again, if they tried to pull me up a slope, I'd just sit down right there and then. I have never got over this problem even today. But what causes it, I have no idea. At other times I don't know what comes over me, I just feel like running - my way and style of course. Dad says I look like a spider from behind, but then what does he know about athletics?

So, walking came late to me, and whenever I have walked I have always had someone with me for safety reasons, even though I have given them a fright at times. Once in a shopping centre I ran off so fast from my daycare carer she couldn't catch me and she had to send a younger, faster carer after me! More good fun. I like these bursts of energy, and often laugh when I have finished running, if only to see the faces of those who are supposed to be looking after me when they catch me.

My best ever experience was with my Dad. He's big and well over 6 foot tall, much bigger than me. Every now and again he takes me to his Nan's grave in South Yorkshire. Whilst there, if I make a lot of noise in the car on the journey, he goes with the flowers to the grave by himself and leaves me in the car, which suits me. But sometimes I forget to make a noise, and we go through the kissing gate together, walk through the graveyard on the path and then have to cross uneven ground to the grave. This upsets me but Dad will insist I go with him. On one occasion with him recently, I wouldn't go to Nan's grave because it was off the flatter path. I began to pull away from Dad as we reached the uneven ground. Trying to cajole me, he pulled me harder. I resisted and grabbed his anorak by the neck, and strengthened my grip on his arm. Dad was not amused and asked me to let go because he was carrying flowers and water for the grave. At first he was polite and then he swore, looking round to see no-one was listening, getting louder and louder. I still held him tight and he dropped the flowers on the floor and in stooping to pick them, up I wobbled on my feet and knocked Dad's glasses off. He couldn't see then and I knew he was getting angrier, at which point I could hear two men shouting to ask Dad if he was all right. They must have thought that while I gripped his neck and held him tight that we were fighting. Dad shouted everything was OK and that I was handicapped. Not at that moment I wasn't, when all of a sudden his anorak came off and I was free – or Dad was. While he picked his glasses up I was off across the graveyard, the two men had gone and Dad was now running after me all red in the face. He caught me after a few yards and took me back to the path where I waited whilst he appeared to throw, dart fashion, the flowers into the vase at the grave. And then we were off. Dad was not happy, and I've had much better car journeys. And I have not been back since to South Yorkshire!

FOOD AND DRINK.

If walking delayed my motor development, then that could not be said about my feeding and eating, which is one of my favourite hobbies. My feeding and diet has provided problems for my parents carers through time. But, so long as my tummy doesn't play up now, as it has done in the past, then things can only be improving.

As a baby I nearly drank my Mum dry of breast milk, and on solids ate for Great Britain. When older, I started to experience problems often frightening people with my loud outbursts of screaming. This was often caused by pain in my tummy, and the only way I could let people know, was, as I said, by screaming. This pain is often of my making because I eat so quickly, and really, if I am not checked, I tend to 'shovel' my food into my mouth. Many have tried to placate me - rocking me, cuddling me, coo cooing to me in an attempt to remove the pain. Try as they might, the pain would not go, and to this day when it occurs, will not go, well not for many hours sometimes. And relief only came via the plumbing systems of the schools or houses I visited with Mum and Dad. And then I began, eventually, to eat my own food with a spoon, and recently, having learnt a new trick, I sometimes use a fork (I have just learned to 'stick' chips with a fork) but never a knife.

My parents also found that even though I am no longer a baby, as long as my food is mashed up into small pieces like minced meat, I have less tummy trouble. So guess what I have loads of? Minced meat in all its guises, but I know they mean well. Similarly there are some foods that, even though they are mashed, still give me problems. These foods are my "red" foods so people know I must never eat them. These include mushrooms, nuts and boiled sweets, to name but a few, and if I eat these by mistake then I am ill, or in pain mainly since I often swallow the foods whole. The foods I can eat, though mashed, Dad has coloured "green". Once, when Dad came to pick me up from a day centre, my carer was angry with me because I had thrown my fish and chips on the floor at dinner time and broken the plate they were on. I had not wanted to do this but no-one had cut up my meal and I couldn't eat it and was hungry. My Dad went mad when he found out, but not with me, with the carers who should have read my care plan.

When I was in my early teens I worked out where my cups were in their cupboards, and when I wanted a drink I would take the cup to an adult, as a hint. Sometimes they took no notice at all, so I just went back, took hold of my blackcurrant juice, and took that to them as well. That nearly always does the trick, particularly when I tilt the bottle! The same goes for cereals: Mum and Dad pester me to get the cereal carton out of the cupboard, go and fetch the milk from the fridge, then get the sugar, then a bowl, and last but not least a spoon. But I am a fast learner and can now gather together most of the necessary drinks or food apparatus before I notify someone, by tugging their arm, that I want to eat or have a drink.

One 'challenge' that I have not conquered is my longing for other people's drinks. Well, they will leave them all over the place and it is so tempting for me, and I cannot help but help myself. They moan and shout at me but I often run off laughing. I once had a bloke shout at me in a pub because I drank his pint of lager, till my carer bought him another pint. Sad thing was - I spilt most of it hurrying to drink it whilst he wasn't watching.

A list of food that I cannot eat at any time, 'red foods', includes all of the following: nuts, raw fruits and vegetables such as apple, pear, strawberry, banana, celery, radish, onion, carrot, cucumber, peppers. Beans, especially baked beans, broad beans, kidney beans, black beans. Peas. Sweet corn. Raw sea food. Muesli. Bean sprouts. New potatoes. Boiled sweets. Mushrooms.

"Green" foods that I can eat are: cooked - rice, pasta, noodles. Cooked vegetables. Scrambled egg. Cooked/stewed fruit. Oranges and some grapes. Well cooked fish and meat. Soups with bread. Cereals of cornflakes, rice krispies, bran flakes. Yogurt/custard. Cake without nuts.

Those that know me will have seen me eat a whole range of food, including some of those in the red zone. But my tummy and digestion is much better, and less difficult if the food I eat comes from the green zone only! And of course, I sleep better.

Sight.

In other ways my development has been quite normal, and possibly along the lines of yours, dear reader. When I was at hospital with Mum on a visit as a baby, the consultant – a Hattie Jacques look-alike - had to test my hearing and sight. Getting behind a screen and prancing behind it, ringing bells from this side and that, had me in stitches as I swung my neck from side to side. Her entourage of students were also wetting themselves with laughter too. All this time I could hear Mum giggling to herself as the silly woman changed bells to try and catch me out. As if? The upshot of this was they declared me to have perfect hearing which I have since been able to demonstrate further with music and aeroplanes. For example, when out in Dad's cars over the years, he has often played tapes of his favourite groups and artists. What he didn't know was that I liked most of the music and remembered it too. So much so, that to show off, I used to tap the tape when the last track of any tape was finishing, and whether Mum or Dad were driving they would then know when to turn the tape over. Good or what? My favourites were Chas and Dave and Mum bought me all their tapes for my enjoyment in the car, but she used to play them quietly to me in my bedroom hoping I would fall asleep at bedtime.

at home 1980

Not only that, but another hobby is aeroplanes, or the noise their engines make. One Sunday morning I stunned everyone at home when I walked from the front of the house to the patio window at the rear of the house just to follow the noise of this big 'bird' in the sky that I had seen. Now I follow all of them from room to room at home, and since that day Mum and Dad have taken me and Anna to all the big airports in England to see the 'birds'. I think the coolest airport is Heathrow because so many of these big 'birds' fly in and out, and to all over the world too, but I'm not really interested in them much if they are on the ground.

When I was tiny my eyesight was very good and I was

able to spot and to pick all the bits of fluff off the floor or a carpet. Some I put in my mouth and was told off. But I could see things on the floor no-one else could, and, by picking them up, I thought I was helping. Anyway, now I have learned to pick up things that I am asked to, by another adult, if I can see what they mean. You see Dad took me to the Brooklands Hospital optician in 2000. After some tests I am sure the optician told Dad I would have to wear glasses. Some hope of that as I cannot stand anything on my head or face and take it, or them, straight off. So I have to get by without glasses. So far so good, especially where my food is concerned! However, I must admit that my eyes have deteriorated with regard to short sightedness, but my long sight seems OK. I can honestly say I can spot an aeroplane in the sky before any of my family. Honest.

Touch.

When I am in a thinking mood I tend to sit quietly and gently scratch myself on my face or head, or under my arms, and even on my tummy. This is so relaxing for me. I often fall asleep afterwards and get wakened by Mum or Dad. The big leather seat they bought for me in the lounge is just too comfy! I touch other people as well, although not to frighten them, just to make them jump. The dog is one target, particularly if she is on my chair. I tap her on the head and she jumps off quickly: sometimes she snaps at me, but she has never bitten me. Dad too, when I don't sleep at night and wander round the landing upstairs flicking the lights on and off. He storms out of his bedroom looking like thunder, and tells me to get back to bed, which I do. Then I do exactly the same again before he asks Mum to vacate her bed and go to my bed. I then have to get in the big bed with Dad. I never sleep though, and when Dad falls asleep I tap him right on his conk, and wake him up and make him jump. He has just told me not to repeat what he says when I do that to him!

Good habit, Bad habit.

While my senses seem to be OK, there are issues that give people cause for concern, and these are really my obsessions. I don't know why it should be, but, every now and then in my life I have felt the need to perform continuous tasks, sometimes from the moment I get up till I go to bed. These tasks often irritate adults, but to me they are routines that I cannot do without. For example, there is the early morning routine which I have always had and still do. In the kitchen, for example, ready for the pre-breakfast cup of tea, out comes the tea caddy, sugar bowl, mugs, milk, teaspoons and sweeteners for Mum. No-one places these objects together in order of size or even in line. They leave them all over the place, higgledy-piggledy and I just feel compelled to re-align them. And this happens with plates, knives and forks, mustard and sauces. In fact, anything that comes out of a drawer or cupboard.

This often irritates my family and others, but for me it is pure Heaven.

It is the same with my routines at toilet-time before school or day centre or unit. Mum and Dad never place the toothbrush, paste, mirror and soap together. My parents are so untidy. And guess what? I then repeat the process all over again before I go to bed. And before I lie down to go to sleep, there is the little matter of the model aircraft, with its large propeller, on the wall above my bed: I just have to rotate that propeller before I lie down to go to sleep, just because it's there, or there is no way I would get to sleep.

I have had some other more nasty fixations in the past. Perhaps my worst was the constant and violent rocking on the floor, on a chair and even in a car. I have no idea what started this habit but I know it became so bad that Mum and Dad used to try and stop me by holding me still, but I only screamed. Boy could I scream! The longer they held me, the louder I screamed, until they let go of me when they were exhausted. At that point I carried on rocking again. Eventually, after what seemed like hours, even I would tire and fall asleep. Some people said I burnt so much energy up, that was why I was so thin. But I never stopped this habit until it became so bad I started to wear away the skin on the palms of my hands and had big sores and blisters on my bottom too. The creams that were applied to the wounds never worked to stop my pain or heal the sores, and eventually, a doctor had to spray some plastic skin on both my hands and bottom. Since then I haven't done much rocking, although Dad says, at the moment in his car, I bounce around as if I am on a trampoline!

Usually when I was rocking from side to side, at home,

I would sit down in the hall. This was a central position in the house downstairs so I could see most of the house from this point. That is, all the rooms and what people were doing because I am a nosey little man and like to keep my finger on the pulse of home life. It was often so busy at my chosen point of control, and that suited my obsession. Mind you, I often had to move out of the way when people were passing through. It was while I was in this position that I started to pull my sleeve up above my elbow. I do this when I go out, even on cold mornings, and I am always being told to pull it down by Mum and Dad. They don't understand, even now, why I do it. Come to think of it, nor do I. Recently I have started to suddenly bend down and touch my shoelaces as I walk at speed, even if someone is guiding me. They are always caught by surprise when I perform this "trick". Still, these habits are hard to get rid of for me, and people like me, and although they may upset or disturb others, for me and my fellow autistic pals they are quite normal.

Two further habits that regularly irk people are my thumb-sucking and my face slapping. The former, I seem to remember, started when I was still a baby, and is part of my routine today. It involves a contortion of my right thumb and first finger. Don't ask me how that began, all I know is that it can be quite 'slobberish' and that is a problem for others, although not me. The number of times I have my hands washed because they smell funny after my habit, is incalculable. However, after a prolonged period of thumb-sucking I do have problems. I suffer from nasty mouth ulcers which really are a pain and purely my fault.

The sucking can be a comfort for me though, which is why I do it, of course. Less understandable to adults is my face smacking which for me only occurs after a period of intense excitement. I can see that others think I am hurting myself, but really the noise is the thing.

When all is said and done, none of my behaviour harms others, or injures them. These individual acts might frustrate people but, after all, they make me the person I am today.

More Obsessions or 'How I can really wind Dad up!'

There are occasions usually when I'm at home, that I get an object in my eye-line which I have to tidy up or re-arrange. Curtains are but one example. In my bedroom, when Mum or Dad put me to bed, I just have to open the left hand curtain. Not the right one mind you, and not the roller-blind Dad put up behind the curtains, to try and fool me. Every time someone closes my bedroom curtains I open the left hand one! The same happens in my bedroom when I am in Respite, the difference being, those curtains are held on with Velcro and they can all fall down with a good yank. The best, and as yet I have not been able to test them, are in the lounge at home: big pink curtains just waiting to be …..! Dad sits next to them so my chances are slim, but I can wait.

These home obsessions really are aggravating for my parents, especially my fixation with cupboard and door handles. It all starts as I enter the kitchen, and I cannot resist opening and shutting the doors there. There are so many: on walls, near the floor, and on the larger doors I just cannot resist tweaking the handles first and then shutting them quickly so the doors bang. All this activity serves to drive my parents 'through the roof' which is fine by me. They'll never understand my needs!

Years ago I used to have the same problem with pieces of string, or wire, or cable I could find. I would just jiggle it about from morning till night. The string I would often put in my mouth and wet it and even if it knotted itself with my jiggling, that was OK. The problems mounted if the string or bendy material was hidden from me. That made me scream or dash round the house searching for that same piece, or any other piece of string. After many years of putting up with this fixation of mine, Dad called in a nurse who had dealt with people like me and my string obsessions. This nurse suggested Mum and Dad reduce, gradually, the length of the string so that I could eventually not jiggle it. This was to stop me in my tracks almost immediately, and after a few screams, I changed my focus to these other obsessions.

In my garden with a bib that has string, 1988

The latest two crazes I have become obsessed with are a variation on my drinking habit. Oh, and I have developed my new 'cough'. Any drink is now a target as I tilt the cup or glass to spill the drink on the floor, or spit out the liquid or gargle when the drink is in my mouth. These latest gags really get a reaction from people and this encourages me even further, as I giggle uncontrollably when they shout at me to stop. Moreover, this gargling has led me to discover a new game of "coughing", or put crudely, "choking". From deep in my tummy I know now how to create panic in the eyes of people as I pretend to choke or sound if I am being sick. This then causes me to laugh uncontrollably as I watch the reaction of the observer. All good fun eh?

The problems that are caused by my obsessions clearly affect lots of people in different ways. This is not deliberate on my part, but is part of my make up. There are other demons I have to confront and these are centred round change: changes to my house where I sleep; to my day centre; respite area and sometimes my diet. These changes all manifest themselves in autistic people in different ways, but when the continuity of their routine exists; they are often at their happiest.

At first I was confused when I transferred school: the teachers and helpers took some getting used to. The buildings and classrooms had different layouts which caused much personal grief. Being able to accept these changes more quickly would have made my life much easier and I'm sure the lives of the persons who looked after me. Then, just as I adjusted to my new school and calmed down, Mum and Dad altered our house, making it much bigger building with a large extension. The building work seemed to take ages: the dust, the noise, the mess and the soil everywhere, all out of place for me to cope with. Too much change like that just blew my mind and I could not settle. I became agitated and noisy: my rocking increased and I certainly needed more string to keep me quiet! This building of house extensions, I know, is difficult for anyone to have to accept, but for the likes of us with autistic tendencies, it is nigh on impossible. Only months after the building was finished, and I was used to the changes, did I become myself again.

Something similar occurred in my first month at the Adult Training Centre (ATC) I attended after being placed with a group of young adults, who, compared with me, were university material. I could not understand the type of work they were doing with paint and brushes as it was all abstract to me. However, I could hear, faintly in the distance, some nice relaxing music. After finding out where it came from, I wandered off to find the source, and succeeded in my quest. The carer in that room let me stay a while, and then I had to return to my own group. I made an impression though and was soon transferred when the Principal thought I was better suited to a room with a calmer, more relaxed atmosphere. In time this changed as more young adults joined the group and the room became too crowded for me, so again I used to absent myself either to the Hall or the garden which I found more tranquil, even in the rain. The staff here tried hard to accommodate me and my foibles, but in the end it simply was a case of numbers: too many for me in one place I'm afraid.

Even my current placement has not been without problems: the autistic group I now share my days with have, since I joined them, had six changes of venue in ten years, and this in a place where they are supposed to understand our needs, in particular the need for continuity. The bonus now is that the clients tend to stay the same, and in the past, so too have the majority of staff. But we are due another move in a couple of months, which I've heard say, should be permanent.

If I could make one plea at this time it is that those persons who are responsible for directing those of us that are autistic must not only be aware of our need for continuity, but also place us in environments where change is the exception rather than a financial move. Why? Because myself, and many of my autistic friends, have been through horrendous times in adjusting to changes and the fallout has been dreadful for all who came/come across us. For example, after some enforced changes I hardly slept a wink of sleep for as much as twelve weeks. This has had untold side effects on my parents' health, and of course my own. I have screamed the place down at home for weeks on end, and following a further meeting with my consultant at Brooklands Hospital, have been put on drugs. I then fought the drugs reactions to my body because I didn't know what was happening to my head and body as they took their effect? When some of these drugs later seemed to clash, nurses told my Mum and Dad that was why I became epileptic and had seizures. Who knows? The seizures don't happen very often though, but they are increasing in number and intensity. Of course I am not aware of these at the time, but I do hear my parents talk about this new and crushing experience for me.

I have described some of my problems in an attempt to let you see what makes me tick. Making me tick is down to my parents, and in their absence, helpers, who have taken over from Mum and Dad, at times, in my development. This has to happen because, apart from feeding myself with fork or spoon, Mum and Dad do everything else for me. My parents always wash, bath or shower me. Then one of them dresses me and prepares my breakfast and later makes sure all my other meals are ready. Dad shaves me better than anyone, and Mum blow-dries my hair like a real hairdresser, all in an attempt to normalise me. Sometimes though my bladder and bowels let me down, especially if I try to get off the toilet too soon! After eating I have Dad clean and brush my teeth - he takes ages and tries hard to make me look like Cary Grant. But that can be too much like hard work for him, because, to be honest, he tries too hard and wracks me off, almost erasing my teeth. But then, bless him, he tries hard to look after my teeth because he knows I grind them a lot when I'm frustrated. Then, last thing at night Mum or Dad puts me to bed, and, of course, I re-arrange the curtains!

Just a normal day in the life of Andrew Miles Gordon

Many times over the last 35 years I have been with my parents to visit doctors in hospitals and surgeries. These have nearly always been as a result of appointments, but occasionally, as the result of an accident I've had too. Tests have been conducted, results given to my Mum and Dad, never to me of course, and if necessary, acted upon in my best interests.

However, one test, without doctors or nurses, or teachers at my schools, was conducted by my parents, just to give them something to do like, one Saturday in April 2006.

This test had a simple aim: to monitor all my activity in a normal day so you can perhaps better understand what I put my family through daily. In one of their observations, to see how active I am, they recorded everything I did for just 10 minutes in one specific period. Not long you might say. But neither Mum nor Dad have shorthand skills, and as you will see, I was really active. Dad says these observations are really typical of any day in my life and follow a pattern that has become a regular feature of my life. If that is so then I'm happy, but I just hope everyone else is too.

This then is the diary, that Mum and Dad kept for that period of twenty four hours, of my behaviour.

Results:

<u>TIME.</u>   <u>INCIDENT.</u>

1.00 am.   Andrew awake on landing, moving about between bedrooms.

1.30 am.   Andrew back in bed.

2.00 am.   Andrew asleep.

4.00 am.   Andrew awake on landing again, running around.

4.00am.+ Andrew visited the toilet– first of 5/6 visits before 5.00am. When towel rings were rearranged several times in the bathroom, the soap put down the toilet with his flannel and eventually his toothbrush. (These are not common occurrences, just today's)

5.00am-6.00am
           Andrew in and out of bed several times.

6.05 am.   Andrew out of bed finally, went to toilet.

6.10 am.   Andrew dragged Mum out of bed, she is not happy.

6.20 am.   Small pot of tea brewed for Andrew, ready to be drunk.

6.30 am.   Andrew's tea all gone. He then looked for more tea in the kitchen.

6.31 am.   Andrew found Mum's tea, despite her hiding it up.

6.45 am.	Andrew found and drank Mum's coffee!!
7.00 am. +	Andrew in shower room being showered. During the next 50 minutes Andrew is dried, dressed and shaved, as are Mum and Dad too! Andrew in lounge, fidgeted around all the time with copper ornaments, papers, books, stools and so on.
7.50 am.	Went out with the "larks" for a walk with Dad. Andrew agitated. Walked OK, but kept on grabbing and pinching Dad's arm. Andrew stopped walking when path was uneven. Dad had to fetch him each time.
8.45 am.	Andrew arrived home. He seemed to thank God. Coats off. Dad prepared breakfast for him and Andrew.
8.50 am.	Until Andrew's breakfast was ready, he opened cupboard doors repeatedly: demanded drinks by placing mugs in front of Mum and Dad; took marshmallows out of plastic container along with crisps, and finally, milk from the fridge. All these were surreptitiously placed in front of one's eyes so as not to miss them!
8.51 am.	Andrew began emptying the mugs, plates and cereal cupboards to speed things along or drop hints? When his bacon and eggs were ready he scoffed the lot in record time, and tried to get some of Dad's. No chance there.
9.45 am.	Breakfast finished.
9.50 am.	Dad went out into the garden.

9.50 am.   Andrew began ferreting around taking tins of soup, beans and tomatoes out of cupboards and in to Mum who was now ironing in the lounge.

9.55 am.   Mum replaced tins in cupboards.

9.56 am.   Andrew appeared in lounge with milk bottle.

9.57 am.   Milk placed back in fridge by Mum.

10.02 am. Andrew took tins out of cupboard again. He wanted fruit and crisps constantly all the time.

11.30 am. Dad returned from garden. Andrew still manic and requiring food and drink from cupboards in kitchen. Continually took mugs to Mum or Dad longing for a drink.

11.45 am. New game started. This involved flicking light switches on and off, first in the lounge, then the dining room, then the kitchen. He must have been sending messages to aliens!

12.00 noon + When he was not doing any of the above Andrew rushed to a toilet upstairs and threw the hand towels in the empty bath, or he ran out of the kitchen to the downstairs loo. Either way, he was not relaxing, reading the Saturday papers as he might have done in different life circumstances.

1.00 pm.   Andrew had 2 Heinz tins of soup and a thick toasted crust for lunch. Then he wanted but did not get custard, jelly and tinned peas.

After lunch the merry go round started again, he wanted Nanny's drink, Mum's cheese sandwich, Dad's sandwich. When these did not happen he went back into the hall and continually removed notebooks from the telephone table and into the kitchen hoping that Mum and Dad would get off their kitchen stools, and then he'd snatch their food.

Dad monitored every move I made for the next 10 minutes and this is what he observed.

At 2.00pm. Andrew flicked lights on and off in dining room and lounge.

Andrew ran to toilet upstairs.

Andrew made squeaky noises.

Andrew switched lights on and off again.

Andrew made humming noises.

At 2.03pm. Andrew ran up stairs again squealing.

At 2.04pm. Andrew ran downstairs to kitchen to remove cereal boxes from cupboard.

At 2.05pm. Andrew squealing in hall.

At 2.06pm. Andrew banged child gate at bottom of stairs.

At 2.07pm. Andrew flicked door handles repeatedly on kitchen door, lounge door, utility cupboard door.

At 2.08pm. Andrew opened and closed kitchen cupboard doors.

At 2.09pm. Andrew made clicking and humming noises at the foot of the stairs.

At 2.10pm. Andrew squealed in kitchen, moved wooden stools across floor, fiddled with door handles.

That short record was made by Mum and Dad for just 10 minutes in an ordinary day with me, Andrew. No wonder I'm so bloody thin!

The next three hours were a complete replica of the monitored 10 minutes above. Mum was in the lounge ironing, and Andrew occupied his usual spot in the middle of the hall, standing or sitting, or running in and out of rooms. When Dad started preparing the evening meal, guess what? I moved into the kitchen to see that my meal was being taken care of too.

Even then I moved objects about: papers, magazines, a biscuit barrel, kettle, fruit bowl or plant pot. I opened cupboard doors and drawers then closed them loudly to create a reaction. When Dad reacted, I just giggled loudly knowing I could play this 'wind-up' game and know the effect it has on Dad. Dad turned the radio on and poured a can of beer and while continuing with the meal, missed a hand stealing his beer. On turning round, Dad saw me pouring the glass of beer down my throat and all down my neck causing Dad to start fuming again. "What a waste of beer" I could see Dad thinking. The cooker hob had its pans re-arranged by me as I grew dissatisfied with their positions my face clearly showing that dissatisfaction.

At 5.30pm the meal, pork chops and apricot sauce with salad, was on the table in the dining room, mine being minced for ease of digestion.

I had finished my meal before the others had taken two mouthfuls, so I then stood up and approached each of the others, "scavenging" for more food. I then moved into the kitchen looking for leftovers. Only then did I return to the table and sit down to eat my pudding, but then left again, leaving the room, loudly shouting and screaming because no-one would allow me some of their food to eat – because, well, they were so slow at eating and I could have helped them.

When the dishwasher was loaded I retired to the lounge and sat down before fiddling with the painting on the wall behind my chair. More fidgeting, moaning, squeaking and thumb-sucking ensued even when the telly was put on for the Lottery Draw and Casualty. As the evening progressed, I closed my eyes and drifted off to sleep, as did my Mum and Dad.

At 10.02pm we all suddenly woke up with a start: the dog was barking. I had a small drink of juice in the kitchen and was taken up to bed and changed into my PJs whilst moving my curtain as usual. Then off to the bathroom for ablutions and teeth cleaning before bed. Here, I got on and off the toilet, peeing on a mat here and the floor there. I was cleaned up and washed and taken to bed. I then moved in and out of bed moving my toy box around the room and flicked my aircraft's propeller just for good measure. But you guessed I'd do that last trick, didn't you?

At 11.30pm all was quiet in my bedroom. Mum and Dad fell asleep, too, before the next day dawned and the whole scenario started again.

Humour.

There have been many sad times in my life: these include the deaths of Nanny Gordon, Grandad Starkings and Grandpops Gordon. These events affected me as they did the other members of my family.

But there is one over-riding ingredient in my family's make-up that helps us survive these traumas and that is our sense of humour. I don't say this lightly, but, we can always find some humour, even at times of tragedy. And boy is it appreciated! Of course, it does not always manifest itself out of tragedy: on many occasions it occurs at someone-else's expense. Now I will try to show how, and why, I laugh so much.

Clearly, humour lightens the atmosphere at times and despite some limitations of understanding, I have been able to appreciate, and develop, my own sense of humour at such moments.

The first time I realised I had a wicked sense of humour was when I was about three years old and found myself rocking on the carpet in the middle of the hall. A Saturday morning at home, wet and raining heavily, which meant that Dad was not refereeing his usual school football match. All the family was in the house at that moment. Mum had disappeared upstairs to collect the tea mugs and bring them down on a tray. Or so she thought! Sliding in her slippers, down 7/8 stairs on her bottom, the tray rattled away with the bouncing mugs, which eventually fell off and continued crashing and bouncing down to the base of the stairs and stopped. Stony silence all round, and for a second further, as Mum followed the tray and mugs down the stairs and also stopped dead still. Meanwhile, Dad zoomed out of the kitchen to see what the racket was all about and found Mum in agony at the foot of the stairs, and me sitting in the middle of the hall. Mum was mouthing words I didn't know and had never heard of or had heard at that time in my life, like 'ooh' and 'blimey' (I think not!) That left me and Dad smirking and trying to control ourselves. It was hopeless and we both failed. Me, I was into uncontrollable fits of laughter, like Dad, and now Mum. My shoulders vibrated as I giggled and laughed, and I should have been crying with laughter, but I don't do tears. My whole body rocked, and for the first time too, not just a smile, but serious tummy-aching laughter. That has now become my trademark posture and reputation. At the instant when some minor trip, accident or fall occurs to somebody, without injury of course, I've noticed that my display of uncontrollable mirth has become infectious and other people react just as I do. Having first tried to hide their laughter, looking round to observe others, they burst out with loud with screams of laughter too. This happens particularly in the presence of my sister Anna, who is a really bad influence on me at these times.

My sense of humour has got me in trouble too, many times, mainly at an inappropriate moment. For example, my laughter and body-shaking can occur when someone sneezes, or when someone shouts or drops something on the floor, or simply makes me jump out of my skin. This does not have to be people in front of me, it can also happen when I am watching television, or listening to the radio. In this camp, two of my favourites that really crack me up are Laurel and Hardy, and the cartoon characters Tom and Jerry. Of course they both have lots of spills and shouting which trigger me off, and then, that's it, me gone, for minutes sometimes. The same is true when fights occur on TV or when boxing is on, or someone is shot in a film or soap, gasping as they go to meet their Maker. Their falling over, their shouts of agony, or deathly squeals are enough to set me off laughing again. Slapstick is a must. Many are the times I should have had tears running down my face as Laurel and Hardy to name but one duo, fall about all over the film set. I look for a reaction in others in the room, and if one isn't forthcoming, I cannot seem to hold myself together anymore. I'm just hopeless. Mum says I take after my Granddad who once, on stepping off a bus, stepped over a woman who had fallen down in front of him, because he was giggling so much. He just apologised and said 'Oops' to her, and never helped her up off the floor. I heard him recall this many times, with tears in his eyes as he did. No wonder I have this appreciation of the ridiculous. My sister Anna is just as bad, if not worse, so it must be in the genes.

To illustrate this wicked humour here is a sample from my Adult Training Centre 'chat book' that clearly shows my wickedness, even when it's me suffering.

'18-5-1993. Andrew very noisy today, distressed at lunchtime and poor Elaine getting the brunt again. Heidi took him to the park for some 1-1 and to feed the ducks. He was OK whilst out – really enjoyed himself – until he tripped and fell over in the park – great hilarity – Heidi said Andrew was laughing in fits on the floor."

There you go, straight from the 'horse's log', so to speak and there is loads more where that came from.

One of the best places to be for a laugh is in Mum or Dad's car: my supposed education has included many Anglo-Saxon words that have added to my 'thinking vocabulary'. Is there any wonder I get funny looks from people I don't know, when I chuckle hysterically as they practise their expletives! The sudden braking of the car can set me off. This happens too when someone cuts up Dad, or pulls out right in front of Mum, causing her to swerve or brake. Out roll the expletives, enough to make a sailor blush. This sets me off again, and even more so when my parents tell me it's not funny. What?

Watching people react is another trigger for my humour. I've been in many large buildings with my family and friends, but the ones I really enjoy are churches and cathedrals. Why? The echo, of course, that is always present in such places. All is very quiet and reverential in these places, that is, until I realise where I am and what is available for me to exploit noise-wise. Suddenly I can emit a holler that is like a train's whistle. 'Ooh, ooh, ooh!' Then all around me people look to see where the noise is coming from. Mum and Dad go bright red and tell me to 'Shush', with me grinning like a Cheshire cat as they come over all embarrassed. It never fails that one.

Another ruse that always works and makes me laugh involves our dog. Merrie, a cocker spaniel, will insist on sitting in my chair when I leave the room for the toilet or whatever. When I return, I look to see if anyone else is watching in their seat, and quietly give Merrie a smack on the head. Not hard, just so she gets off my chair. But the pay-off is when she barks at me, and that is what causes the reaction of others in the room, who, if they have been asleep, jump to it and ask what the problem is.

Merrie the dog

But the best incident of all, at least gauging by my family's and friend's reactions over the years, involved me and Dad, in the car, on a red light at a set of traffic lights. Several Hell's Angels on big bikes, arrived simultaneously on Dad's left, my passenger door. I must remind you here that I still suck my thumb and my first finger, on the same hand, and at the same time. When I take these out of my mouth I often fashion my first and second fingers in a V-shape. So, there we are at the lights, and this big, big ugly man sees me flicking my V-shaped fingers, in his direction, and signals to some of his mates what he has seen in the car next to him. These blokes are so big, unshaven, dirty, and with only bits of pink skin showing through their tattoos. They probably open tins of beans with their teeth! Fortunately, one of them saw my disabled badge in the car, signalled to his mates that it was nothing to bother about, and so as the lights turned to green, they sped off and left Dad standing, as if we were being overtaken by a Saturn rocket! Dad was quiet on the way home and spent a long time in the loo soon after arrival, telling Mum how close we came to being eaten, I think. Anyhow, this incident, on being told many times, has given us lots of laughs. But Dad was not laughing at the lights that morning!

ANDREW GIVE US A KISS

Practicing for the Hells Angels? 1975

Relieving pressure helps in our situation and what better way to do it than with humour? Mum and Dad, along with me and Anna have had loads of laughs down the years, and still do. I suppose it keeps us all sane?

Thank you to all my Friends and Carers.

I must now find a way, somehow, to thank all of those family, friends, teachers, social workers, carers, nurses and doctors, who have, over the last 35 years helped me, and Mum and Dad, in making our life much easier than it might have been.

In attempting the above, I realise that I may have neglected to thank people on my journey through life. I apologise unreservedly if I have done so, but this has been unintentional.

So many people have been involved in my life, especially in my first few hours when Mum and I nearly did not survive. There are those, also, who have been heavily involved in my development too, and in caring for me, and their level of help and commitment must have far exceeded their work done with normal children. This all seems so long ago, I sometimes wonder if it happened at all.

Clearly, on the medical side, the first people to thank are the doctors and nurses who were there at my birth at Marston Green Hospital, and helped Mum with her side of things. They were obviously skilled in dealing with an emergency, which I was. On top of that, the usual paraphernalia in sorting out the registration of birth, monitoring of my jaundice, and helping Mum adjust to my bathing, washing and feeding, was all done by lovely nurses who just made Mum's experiences with a new baby easier.

Community nurses from the local clinic, who were involved in my early months, despite trying to convince Mum I was lazy, were only trying to make her and Dad not lower their sights about me. And after consultants concluded that I had a problem, they were eager again to help my parents.

Good Hope Hospital was to become a focus for much of my early life, as I have previously mentioned, whilst my early developmental assessments were conducted there. These, although very serious, some were often conducted with what appeared to Mum to be great humour. Although I have mentioned this incident previously, I think it is totally relevant to recall it here. My humour became evident when my 'sight and hearing' were tested, behind screens, with noisy toys, by a rather large lady and her students. Punch and Judy spring to mind as an example of that lady's energy. Wow!

The staff at Good Hope Hospital have always been good to me, whether I have visited for surgery, patching up, or routine blood tests over the years. When I was three

I had two hernias operated on, and as it was my first time in hospital, they let Mum stay overnight with me. Later I broke my leg and had it plastered really quickly, jumping the queue, I think, because of my disability. Mum was so pleased with their efforts, I know because she sang their praises to Dad. Similarly, visits for blood tests or check ups, have always been conducted by staff that then afforded me respect and dignity, and treated me no differently from other children.

My local doctors' practice for over 30 years has been very accommodating allowing me to wait outside, in the car park, rather than sit in the crowded waiting room which would have driven me barmy. Then, when a pre-arranged signal to Mum or Dad was sent, they let me in the backdoor, clandestinely of course, to visit the doctor or nurse. And in all that time I have never felt a 'jag' of the needles I've had stuck in me! As recently as this last July 2006, I gave Mum and Dad a fright, on the day of Mum's retirement party at home, by drinking gallons of juice and the occasional 'vino' in an attempt to relieve what seemed like an unquenchable thirst at the time. My sister Anna tested my blood and found the blood sugar reading far too high. So the following morning I was marched off to the doc's for more tests which were, thank God, eventually to prove negative. However, the empathy shown to me by the young doctor and very attractive nurse, were really appreciated by all of us at the time. More by way of relief I suppose.

This same doctors' practice has a health centre at the rear, which over the years has sanctioned requisitions for various bed sheets and nappies to help with my incontinence. It was here Mum met a nurse who suggested, several years ago now, that I do away with the padded paper and plastic sheets on my bed and use, instead, a more beneficial and washable under blanket-like sheet. A bit clinical at this point, I know, but it illustrates the technological advances, in my lifetime, of the dear old bed-sheet. And it makes Mum's job a bit easier if I have an accident.

Whilst dealing with hospitals at this juncture, it is convenient to mention Brooklands Hospital where I currently receive my day care, and incidentally my respite. In 1993 I had a particularly bad patch in my life. So bad that I had a prolonged period of assessment at Brooklands, which at one stage I thought I would never get away from, my state of mind was so bad at that time. That assessment continued, periodically, with a few breaks, into 1995. Dr Ashok Roy, who has been my psychiatric consultant, for twenty years now, has played an increasingly vital role in my development and rehabilitation. This has involved consultations with Mum and Dad, and prescribing and the administering of any medication necessary when I had at times been really disturbed in 1993. During this period, Mum and Dad could not cope with my severe and challenging behaviour. My constant shouting and screaming, my charging about the house, my total lack of sleep which often lasted for weeks on end, my return to quite bad incontinence, slamming of doors and other changes to my self-control, that really would have tested the patience of a saint, certainly tested Mum and Dad to exhaustion. Help was needed urgently, and hence the need for both Dr Roy and Brooklands.

At this same time I was to suffer the first of several bad injuries which drove my parents ballistic. Whilst I was being assessed, a client obviously did not like me and almost bit my nose off my face. Fortunately, the doctors at the Heartlands Hospital, East Birmingham, were able to repair the damage and I returned to Brooklands to continue assessment that night. My Mum was beside herself, as was Dad, mainly I think because I have few, if any, emotions, and despite the horrid nature of the injury I was not unduly concerned. The other client, thank God, was given a 24 hour 'guard' for the rest of my time there, and so I came to no further harm.

Later, I was badly bitten by a client but it was my fault for nicking his tea. I also went on to have my nose broken three times at Brooklands: once with a black-eye that unbelievably, was given me by one of two members of staff! Needless to say, they were removed and aren't supposed to work in the NHS again. They had claimed I was injured by a fellow client who reportedly caught me with his knee, in my face as he ran passed me whilst I was rocking on the floor. I should coco! My Dad was nearly arrested for what he said he would do to the two blokes who had assaulted me if he got his hands on them, when he and Mum visited the police station for the CPS results. Even the Detective Inspector who spoke to Dad blushed, and Mum certainly did because she is a lady! I cannot tell you either what Dad said when the CPS would not take the thugs to court "because the witnesses to the assault could not speak either". Let's just say you could be jailed for thinking the words Dad used to the policeman who was brave enough to tell him there was no case to answer for my assault.

Another break on my nose occurred a year later, again when I was in respite. Undetected by staff on that Saturday morning my 'old man' came to pick me up, and Dad spotted the broken nose immediately. That's it so far regarding my injuries to date, and I hope that they are finished with. Except to say the surgeon at Heartlands Hospital who attempted to straighten my nose had to leave me with what he called a 'ski-lift' nose because he couldn't straighten it anymore during a remedial and reconstructive operation fairly soon after that last break.

Gradually, and with lots of support, I recovered, not only from my injuries, but also from the disturbed behaviour I had exhibited. Although I was not yet behaving like Lord Fauntleroy immediately, I gave enough indication to suggest that I could be one day.

Whilst I was in Brooklands being assessed in 1995 I added to my medical condition by having an epileptic seizure. Apparently I answer to the Tonic Clonic set, which I must confess, when I first heard that description, I thought it was a drink. I seem to have a seizure once a month now, and their frequency is increasing as I get older. At the moment, I do not take medication for my seizures, but this is under consideration as I write. I haven't a clue when these seizures are about to happen, only that I wake up very tired and want to go to sleep. So far, apart from one seizure, all have been in the early morning. It was also at this time in 1995, that my father became very ill, so much so we nearly lost him twice, and then had to retire from teaching, which he has not stopped moaning about since.

Brooklands, meanwhile, has also overseen other details of my life: I have been to a hairdresser on site during stays; I have had my eyes tested and was told I would need glasses for short-sightedness. I have also visited the dentist who on one famous occasion arranged for me to be 'knocked out' so he could fill some of my teeth: he took out all my wisdom teeth instead! The thief! On the way home from the hospital that day, after an hour and a half recuperation – it should have been four hours – Dad was so proud of me in the car on the way home, he kept smiling and telling me what a brave bloke I was.

I must record that the staff at Brooklands have been my lifeline in day care for ten years now, and the progress I have been able to make socially is also greatly down to them. They walk me miles they do, they take me everywhere in the mini-buses, they feed me loads, and they look after me in respite. They are, at this moment, my second family and second home. I cannot name them all, but can only thank them for the time and effort they have put in with me and on my behalf, and on behalf of my parents.

When my behaviour was so disturbed in the Nineties, Individual Care Services from Redditch, Worcestershire, became heavily involved with helping me to modify my conduct. They provided support on a one-to-one basis with me 4 days a week, and still do to this day, at Brooklands. Really, it is another pair of eyes keeping me on the straight and narrow! And Dad says it works, so there is always a big thanks for their staff.

Education.

Throughout my life Mum and Dad have had incredible support from the staff in the schools they worked in, initially before I was born, and especially after my condition was diagnosed. The Head teachers were always so helpful, in allowing Dad mainly, to have time off so that we could attend the various clinics, surgeries or hospitals, together, as and when became necessary. By allowing this, this simple generosity enabled Mum and Dad to spend more time together to come to terms with the complexities of my condition which would of course change their lives forever. The staff in these schools, too, became a comfort and source of support for the whole family and again, in their way, lightened the 'load' further for my parents. Mum and Dad tell me they used to get lots of offers from staff to baby sit Anna and me. Pupils used to offer to baby sit too, and many used to come and visit our house when we lived close to the school. On several occasions Dad took me and Anna into school with him and told stories about us to the pupils in his Year assemblies. Sitting in front of a whole year of 300 pupils was nerve racking I can tell you.

During all this time, Mum has had the support from staff in a different form: she has raised, with their help, thousands of pounds by selling Xmas cards and donating all the profit from them to the various schools, societies or day centres I have attended. This year was her 24th year of raising this type of funding. The whole staff at

Smiths Wood School have been tremendously supportive of Mum's fundraising over many of these years and we are forever grateful to them for that support.

My school education began, for a short time, at Merstone School, Solihull, but when we moved to Sutton Coldfield I transferred to the Bridge School, Erdington where I stayed until I was 13 years old. I'm not really sure who enjoyed the experience more, me or Mum and Dad. Me perhaps, because the school was really like a home from home, or maybe Mum and Dad because they could see me making progress and I was settled there and happy too. Hence my parents were able to relax a bit more and get on with their lives, in the knowledge that I was safe.

Whilst there Mum used to dress me up every now and again in fancy paper hats as big as kings' crowns. The first time this occurred was for the Queen's Jubilee in 1977, and they tried to make me wear the fancy hat all day, and take pictures of me. The best thing at these celebratory events was always the food: as much as you could eat, and more. I often needed a bath after some of these occasions when I'd filled my face, missing my mouth or plastering my nose with creams or jam.

I think too, that I began to enjoy all kinds of music at this school for the first time, outside of my home. The soothing nature, the rhythms, the notes and tunes all became a part of me and clearly helped to relax me. Loads of times I requested that the teachers replay the music, or pushed a radio towards them so they might switch it on. But the greatest treat was to be able to get to the piano, shuffling on my bottom, or later, walking in a wobbly fashion, straight to the piano and its keys. Here I plinked and plonked away totally out of tune, or by taking the teacher's hands and pushing them to the keys! Whatever, I got my beloved music. Further more in this school, if I didn't feel I'd had enough to eat at lunchtime, I could wander off to find one particular teacher who always had salad and a sandwich for her lunch and she would feed me some of hers too. What a creep I was, learning how to be nice to ladies, in order to get my own way. And I was handicapped.

1976 Easter Bonnet – Thanks Mum!

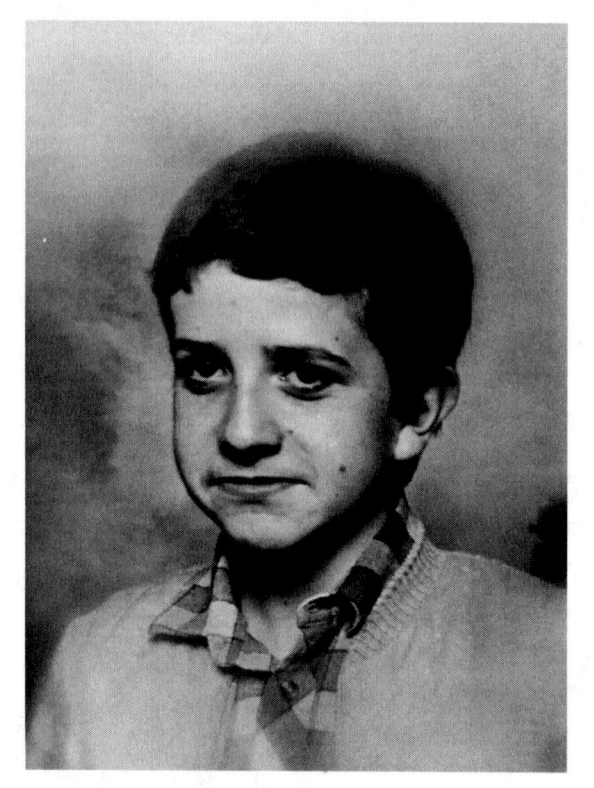

Bridge School 1984, just before I left

It was a sad day when I left this school to attend the big pupil's school: but only because Bridge School had become part of me, made me happy, made me smile and had really helped me so early and caringly in my life. The wrench was not helped with my onset of puberty, and the school being so much bigger than my last school. I got taller too and became more of a handful, and not the well-behaved smiling baby face I had been previously. But Kingstanding School wasn't the problem. It was me who was changing, growing up and developing my own personality, so much so that I even started to be shaved. I went out more here in school time, visiting farms and horse-riding. Horse riding became a problem for me when it was realised I was allergic to horse hair and I had severe problems with my eyes. (and the same later occurred at the seaside with donkeys.) I even went away with the school for a week's holiday to Sheringham, Norfolk: I bet my parents were not half glad of the break.

I remember, too, while I attended Kingstanding School and whilst my walking was improving, going shopping one Saturday morning with Mum and Dad in Sutton Coldfield. It was the first time I'd been without my big wheelchair and Dad and I were standing outside Woolworths waiting for Mum who was in the store. Standing there, Dad noticed some young men laughing at me. They had leather jackets on, and one gave a funny salute. Needless to say Dad was 'airborne' again, and moved ten yards towards them remonstrating with these scum, only to realise he'd left me on my own, and so gave the chase up as a bad job. But he would not let up his tirade at these thugs. Berating these young blokes from a distance, he eventually gave up and went round the corner, a few streets away, to his mate Simmo to continue the discussion with me in attendance, I thought Dad was going to explode. However he quietened down when Mum arrived on the scene. Mum calmed him down, as usual – and we all went home, had lunch, and the moment passed – I think! But you never know with Dad, sometimes he can ...

At Kingstanding School the staff tried very hard to press on with my educational and social development. Here I was to be cajoled into using computers, which I never got the hang of, and painting and art work from one member of staff who was an artist in her own right. I spent most of my time here with this same teacher, who tried very hard with me in all educational directions, but I just wasn't interested most of the time. Break time and a drink, lunchtime and the food were my main essentials, and of course, the bus home. But my Mum and Dad enjoyed the time I had here, so it was easier for me too, until that was, when I had to move to an Adult Training Centre, ATC.

This transition was made that much easier for me as I had afternoons, a whole day and a 2-day induction period to adjust to a different culture, before I started full time. This induction at least allowed me to get used to the change of venue gently, from school to ATC. I even had to attend an interview, but Mum and Dad answered the questions and so I just wandered out of the interview room despite Dad's attempts to 'imprison' me there! Ultimately I attended Ebrook ATC full time, and even though there were hiccups to begin with over transport, these were eventually sorted. The ATC opened after the time of day Mum and Dad should have been teaching, so, with the ATC, they negotiated that I be dropped off each day, before 8.00am. at '76 Holland Street', a residential home for people like me. A taxi then took me and other students to Ebrook where, at first, I had to work for heaven's sake! Gosh, the rest of the group I was with, compared with me, were all working on their PhDs. They could paint, crayon, cut out shapes with scissors and dance in time to music just for starters. Me? All I wanted to do was listen to some calming music, be restful and peacefully quiet and generally just contemplate my navel. Some hope.

Well I did have many happy times in the ATC, many more than the bad times, although in the end I became very disturbed with this first group and my own inability to perform simple tasks. I therefore needed to transfer elsewhere. Initially, this group I was with , as I have mentioned, were far ahead of me in skills work. The painting and craftwork were so beyond me I had difficulty coping, and so it was when I heard music coming from across the main hall, I wandered off to find its source. And when I did, they let me in to stay and listen. This was to become permanent eventually, but at the beginning they kept escorting me back to my original group, after a short stay in their company. I was desperate to join this lovely peaceful, quiet and tranquil group so I persisted absconding from group one, and fortunately for me, they gave in, and I transferred groups, eventually.

I was so happy at the beginning in this new group: there was quiet, or music, only a few clients and me, and some lovely ladies who were polite and charming with all of us. In this group there were visits out to the gym for badminton and table tennis, (Huh?) and other trips out in the centre bus, often to the shops. This routine carried on for four more years with me only having time off to attend the assessment unit at Brooklands Hospital. As I have said earlier, these assessments were because of my vastly deteriorating and challenging behaviour at home and at Ebrook.

Some of this may have been down to my intolerance of increasing numbers of clients and staff in my group's room. That said, the help and care that the staff always gave to me was always first rate. There were no raised voices, only their kindness and pleading with me to alter my ways. All their help was to no avail of course because of my challenging behaviour. In fact matters began to escalate after a certain Friday in the Dining Hall. Someone forgot to cut up my fish and chip lunch into small pieces. I certainly had no chance of doing that myself, so I became confused, and then angry. In my desperation, I responded by throwing the dinner plate across the room, pushed chairs out of my way and stormed into the garden shouting and screaming for some peace.

This single incident, more than any of the others, convinced Mum and Dad, that my placement in this ever more increasingly crowded day care centre, for me was wrong. In the meantime, at every opportunity I was leaving my group to sit in the un-crowded and "quiet garden", come rain or shine. Further ammunition, if it were needed, was the knock-on effect my misbehaviour was having on my family. Not wanting this episode to continue, Mum and Dad decided I had to be removed voluntarily from Ebrook, before I was perhaps asked to leave. None of my problems could be laid at the feet of Ebrook staff: they had tried their best with increasing numbers of clients. And the problems were solely my inability to cope with crowds or crowding. So, thanks to the Ebrook staff for trying to help me and also for their help in getting me re-housed elsewhere so quickly. All this of course precipitated my move to Brooklands and a special day care arrangement, for me and other autistic people, which I am still currently attending and have been since 1997.

Partying.

People have often stopped to ask my parents how I am progressing socially or educationally, or even if I am sleeping properly and sometimes, even, if I have I been out. You know - the 'Does he take sugar?' questions? And I can honestly say, in answer to all the questioners, I have led a varied and sometimes, even for me, exciting life. Clearly much of this has stemmed from my social life which I shall endeavour to enlighten you about in the next few pages.

Apart from visiting Mum and Dad's friends or family or them visiting us, much of my early social contact, away from school, was with members of the Centre of England Society. This existed to raise the profile of handicapped children in North Solihull, (Chelmsley Wood), or the surrounding area, and the main stalwarts of this brilliantly run society, were Mary and Tony Crowther.

Many of the activities arranged by the society, on behalf of the children, were fully thrashed out in their committee meetings. I know this because Mum and Dad were soon elected, 'to the committee' and served for years, and were always chuntering on about things. Most, but not all, of the committee members, were parents of a handicapped child, but all were active in raising funds, supporting events, or helping to arrange the varied and exciting events, trips and parties. These would include Xmas parties, trips to the seaside or inland centres, sponsored walks, and last but not least, the August Bank Holiday stall at the Coleshill Carnival. This was the highlight in the whole of the social calendar and a main fundraising event.

Meanwhile, the Xmas parties were legendary. The aim for the children was to spot who was the Father Xmas. Or rather, which adult was now missing from the milling throng as kids jostled for position to receive their gifts. Siblings, too, received a present and the funding was so good that the presents were really worth having. So there we all are at this annual party, in our wheelchairs, or whatever, the music blaring out – no-one dancing, at that moment, just ladies dashing everywhere with sandwiches, cups of tea, juice, cakes and biscuits, the like of which is only ever assembled at do's like this or when the war ends. Children are everywhere, the stolen trifle a dead giveaway on their 'chops', and just as the noise and music reach bursting point, there is this loud West Yorkshire accent announcing that 'tea is served!' Tony had spoken, in his best Chairman's voice, and the first scrimmage began to move towards the food: the second scrimmage was that of the parents, who like their children, appeared not to have eaten since the previous Xmas! Me, I just waited for my

Mum or Dad, and later when she was bigger, my sister Anna, to bring me food. That way I never lost out, and if I rejected something off the plate, I knew someone who always finished it up, didn't you Dad?

Mum always knew that after the Xmas party, usually held in January and in a hostelry large enough to have a function room for the fathers to drink in, that the next committee meeting would select the full day and half day trips out for that year. These days out were always on a Sunday, and the committee's decision always depended on how long it had been since they had previously visited the seaside resorts in question. This was always a real slog, the selection of venue, that is, according to Mum. Why? Because those who had been in the society at its start had been to every seaside, not once but several times. Weston-Super-Mare, Rhyl, Prestatyn, Blackpool, Morecambe, Southport, Cleethorpes, Skegness and all motorway stops on the way. These "comfort" stops were hysterical not only for the length of time spent in the service areas – never enough for the ladies – but we always seemed to be there nearly as long as we were at the seaside. Then when the 3 or 4 buses arrived at the venue, the process of handing out the pocket money, for the handicapped child in the family, began. How much the actual child saw I have no idea, but I know this, I got all mine cos my Mum told me so.

Going round some of these places though, particularly when it was raining, was an education. Often the nearest chippie, or pub, or amusement park, were some families' main objectives, and sometimes for the whole of the day out. There wasn't any chance of me being allowed in somewhere like that though for my amusement. Oh no, I was often traipsed through the rain in search of fresh air and ozone to clear my head and nostrils!

These lovely days out caused more hilarity at going home time. Tradition dictated that Chairman Tony, and his mate Bob, had to have a pint back at their local pub as soon as they arrived back home, preferably by 8.30pm. So woe betide anyone who delayed our departure!

Sometimes families were almost left behind if they did not get back to the coach on time. Tony would be on his 50th fag, turning beetroot red, and blowing a gasket at the thought of being late to the pub.

Once we had begun our journey home, motorway service "comfort breaks" caused further despair. I swear half the women never got near a toilet seat before Tony was ranting on again. I mention this because Mum and Dad always giggled and saw the funny side of these things. After all the hard work fund raising, and it was hard work, and Mary and Tony worked harder than anyone else, here were scenes of comedy that would have gone down well at the cinema. It certainly was becoming slapstick by the minute and loads of people laughed. I loved the tension, smiling every time someone was berated by Tony or Bob, just for making them old buggers late for a pint of beer.

Whilst the raising of funds for the society was of paramount importance in order to provide parties, trips, pocket money and presents for the children, anyone who, in or out of the society, raised money legitimately, was welcomed by the committee with open arms. This was the case with a young teacher who worked with Mum and

Dad. Roger Airey ran three London Marathons on behalf of the children in the society, raising hundreds of pounds in the process. People like him, who do not have problems as Mum and Dad have with me, really are the angels in our midst and we children are really grateful to them. Thanks Roger for all of your incredible support.

Terry Coates, an old boy of Dad's, raised over £500 in an open day at his firm, which went a long way to paying for several 'seaside' coaches one Sunday Trip.

The society really did work for the children in the local area, and I am sure that children like me fully benefited from the expertise of the people on that committee. Mum eventually served as treasurer for 14 years, and Dad did 8 years as chairman, but only left when I became ill in the Nineties. At the time the money side was flourishing, but, sad to say, that, following bereavements, and the passage of time, the society no longer exists. I bet Tony and Mary are turning in their graves.

Friends and Family.

There are many friends whom I have grown to love and appreciate in my life. I have spent long periods of time with some of them, for one reason or another. This may have been in a daily capacity at Brooklands in the form of Individual Care Services (ICS), or in two different forms of respite, nightly, or for weekends and longer stays.

All these friends have paid me total respect and always maintained my dignity, even when I have been difficult and very trying, to say the least. The ICS staff I first met in Brooklands following my illnesses, helped me 'calm down' and readjust my behaviour. These people took me out walking, to McDonalds, Burger King, or pub restaurants and garden centres simply to help me be a little less distressed. Sometimes the ploys worked, and even when they were not so successful, at least the car ride was worth it. I've been to shopping malls all over Birmingham; to theme parks; airports; railway stations, and up and down main roads so many times I could be a tour guide for the

West Midlands Tourist Office if I could talk. I have even had the pleasure of sitting in a cabriolet (a posh car with the hood down) with the wind in my hair, feeling a right toff as I was driven through the countryside. The time these friends spend making me the centre of their day for the period I spend in their company is special for me, and that is why they are all my special friends.

Other friends have included Mary and Peter Whittle, from the Birmingham Multi-Handicapped Group, who, from the time I was 9 years old until I was 18 years old, came to sit and look after me and Anna, enabling Mum and Dad to go out together for a few hours. They mainly went to functions at their school or meetings for the handicapped, and sometimes they'd go for a drink with friends. But always Peter and Mary would help if they could, and they have stayed in touch with me to this day. Sadly, Mary recently passed away, but she and Peter will remain firm favourites to all my family.

Another lovely lady, from the same organisation, is Nel Reid, who took over from Mary and Peter, and I see her most Thursdays, again when Mum and Dad venture out on to the streets of Brum. Nel is Aston Villa barmy, and goes to see them at the drop of a hat. Having said that, Nel recently gave up her season ticket at Villa Park, just as the team have begun to revive and make progress. She must be 'under the moon' and "sick as a parrot" with regret. Again, Nel has been a good friend to me, one whom I cannot do without at the moment and I really appreciate the time and effort she puts in for me and my family.

Some other friends I used to go and stay with for the

occasional weekend, or a week or two at holiday times, and even made a TV commercial with, are Dennis and June Flaherty, and their daughter Sue and son Steven. Staying with June was like living with a whirlwind and hurricane; she never stopped moving or working until her bedtime, and she expected me and her kids to be the same. I ask you. Cooking, gardening, playing games indoors or out, no wonder I needed a holiday when I left her home for my own home. But the enthusiasm and care were remarkable, and she is only knee high to a grasshopper too. But there was never any doubt who was the boss with June around, that was for sure.

When my old taxi firm could no longer take me to school, Mum or Dad dropped me off at Dennis and June's, and Stevie's taxi driver took us both to and from our school. But even all that came to a very reluctant end for me. As I grew taller, and stronger I made it impossible for June to control me as she needed to. Basically I became too stroppy, just like my Dad. So my parents had to re-negotiate a different deal for me, and that's how I came to be at '76 Holland Street' and attended Ebrook Adult Training Centre (ATC), just less than a mile away.

'76 Holland Street' is a Birmingham City residential home for the handicapped. Here I was dropped off by my parents in the morning and left with the other clients so they, Mum and Dad that is, could go to school. One of them would pick me up again at night, and I even began eventually to have the occasional weekend's respite there too. This arrangement worked all the way through my time at the ATC, and when I finished there to attend Brooklands full time in 1997, I finished staying at '76 Holland Street'.

At Brooklands, the venue has changed, building wise, on several occasions so far, but neither the clients nor the staff have changed much, and most of them have been my friends now for over ten years.

This need for continuity of service input, in all its forms, and the knock on effect it has for helping autistic people, cannot be overstated. The need for regular patterns in daily life, for example, is paramount for our health and well-being. Earlier I described how, when these patterns in my own life were broken, I became agitated, noisy, angry and very disturbed, depending on how long the break occurred. One factor that certainly helped me and my family at those times of my challenging behaviour, was the regularity with which close friends were soon on the scene, offering either to help with me, or to make life easier for Mum and Dad. From my point of view I cannot thank those people enough in helping us all, and not only in troubled times, but for their support throughout my life.

At the beginning of my development, and during that difficult time for my parents, Dominick and Mary Campbell, through living close to Mum and Dad, were always on hand to take Mum and I to appointments, either at hospitals fifteen miles away, or to the clinic, particularly if it was raining, because Mum and Dad did not drive a car at the time of my birth. And we went to loads of other places too in their old Ford Anglia, one of the few to have hardly any flooring, so you could see the road under the car! But that was not all. Dominick and Mary had been very productive at bringing children into this world. 'Wee' Dom, Ewan-Francis and James, were all born in the space of three years and they too used to accompany Mum and I in the Campbell car - so it was just one big party as Mary drove us to wherever we had to go. This early close friendship my parents had with Dom and Mary certainly helped them when the results of my tests were appearing on the doormat at home in the post from the hospitals and clinics. And there was many a time when the four adults talked until all hours late into the night as the inquests began as to my medical condition. Sadly for us they moved back to Scotland, and although they had another child, a daughter Maria, after Dominick's promotion in teaching, we have only visited them on a few occasions. But they always call in when they have come down to England, often but not always, en route to France. Sad to record then that just before Xmas 2005, 'Wee Dom' died in his sleep after losing an ongoing battle against a medical condition which finally took its toll.

Dom, Andy, Ewan 1973

Even further back in time, before I was born, and when both Mum and Dad were at college, they formed a friendship with a guy, Stewart Cooper, who eventually went on to teach with Dad in two schools. 'Stew' is my Godfather and he and his wife Teresa have been close family friends to this day. Regular visits are made, home or away, with their daughters Emma and Sarah, despite a fair mileage between the two family homes. The swapping of birthday treats and Xmas presents has always been fun for me because of the long car ride to their house. Each time we meet now, Mum and Dad seem to be carrying on conversations with 'Stew' and Teresa as if they had left the last conversation hanging on a comma. That's how close I see their friendship, and again, 'Stew' and Theresa have always lent a good ear for my parents.

Moving on, the friends who have had the most influence on me, throughout my life are, without doubt, 'Uncle' Ian, affectionately known as "unclean", and 'Aunty' Nette. Ian taught with Dad from 1974, and soon after Nette moved to the Midlands from Luton, and we were all introduced. I was just two years old at the time and soon was aware that new faces were in and around the house, with different 'suveners accents loike'. Slowly the friendship with them gelled and when we moved house they played a major part in helping us move, and make the new house ready, and fit for purpose. And this even though the door handles all seemed to open either upside down or back to front.

Over the next few years I was to see more and more of them: we went on holiday several times together.

Sometimes there were others in the group too. The first time I remember only too well because it was in a tent on the Gower Coast in Wales. Of course I was up all night with Mum, me screaming in the car because I could not digest new potatoes, and Mum with her hand over my mouth, trying in vain to quieten me. The second time we all holidayed together was on a barge for a week in 1976. That's right, the year of the big drought and when the canal water was reduced massively in the "cut". It was so hot that year and they kept perching me on the roof of the barge so I could enjoy the views! But I reckon it was to watch the blokes drinking. So many funny incidents occurred on this holiday it is easier to understand JK Jerome's book, 'Three Men in a Boat' now. Ian and Nette were to go on loads of holidays with Mum and Dad after that, all over Europe, North America and Alaska, and Dad took Ian to a Test Match in Cape Town one year, such was their friendship. If they self catered, Dad drove the car; Ian was "navigator" and directed him; Nette was the "purser" (she's Scottish!) and Mum always wrote a diary so they had a record of their time on holiday.

For weeks, after we moved house, these friends came to us on many Sunday nights and had supper and played cards with Mum and Dad. So raucous was the laughter from the dining room, as they played cards, it's a wonder me and Anna ever slept. I just know that Mum and Dad enjoyed the visits which acted, in a healing sort of way, to lighten their emotional load that arose with my condition.

On a couple of evenings we had two phone calls, and

from the way Mum and Dad ran around, those on the other end of the phone line must have been desperate. The first from Nette after Ian had cut his head by walking into the garage door. (Too much red wine I suspect.) Dad took him to hospital and Ian had several stitches inserted in his wound. But on another night, not to be outdone, Ian, having had the Mickey taken out of him by Nette about his accident, had the last laugh. Nette herself had to have stitches in a badly cut finger, having been bitten by her dog Sheena! This, after she had tried to remove a spare rib bone from the dog's mouth! This time Mum took Nette to hospital, and for the most part they both laughed at how the injury had occurred.

There were countless other occasions when we all met, and Ian and Nette supported Mum and Dad. Several of these involved my sister Anna, who, if she was into a bad hypoglycaemic attack, sometimes had to go to hospital with Mum or Dad to help sort her Type 1 diabetes. No surprise then that, following a phone call to Ian and Nette, they were always there to look after me, day or night. Further, when Dad was in hospital for some time they visited him every day and when he returned home to recuperate. They even walked me round the cricket field whilst Dad was playing for his club, Coleshill, and fed me my tea as Mum prepared the cricket teas. I went to birthday parties at their home – they never missed me out from any social gathering. I heard them on some occasions, nearly always at Xmas in particular, knock on our door late at night as they left Dad to face Mum's wrath. This was nearly always after drunken nights at the cricket club, even after carol concerts would you believe? There was many a time Dad came into the house late at night noisily, only to find Mum fast asleep in bed ignoring him. But, on other occasions, when he arrived home quietly without a sound, there was Mum waiting with the rolling pin! I wonder to this day how on earth she knew.

But perhaps the time I was most grateful for their help, and Ian's on this occasion, was at Anna's wedding to Mike. I was really dressed up to the 'nines': morning suit, proper frilly shirt, waistcoat, bow tie, fancy shoes I really looked the mutt's nuts. But could I stand the waiting around, the photographs, the whole wedding scene, and all those people? Not a chance. Maybe if they had dressed me in mufti I'd have coped. I stomped and shouted, screamed, and rocked violently when sitting on the floor, and became so unpleasant that I had to be taken out of the hotel into the gardens. Still I never settled, not even with Dad in attendance, and with the wedding meal just about to start. Dad was apoplectic. No need to worry though, as 'Uncle' Ian rode to the rescue again, took me home, fed me, settled me down, toileted me, and only then began to relax himself. He did that with one of Dad's best red wines!

That was the man: a real friend who would do anything to help someone less fortunate. It was therefore, a massive shock when this lovely friend of ours became ill and died of lung cancer in 2005. I've never seen Dad so upset, but what would you expect? Uncle Ian had become the brother Dad never had, and such a good 'Uncle' to me and Anna. I know he looks out for me from beyond the clouds. 'Aunty' Nette still comes round regularly, and she and mum go to London with the 'girls' now and then. They have all been on holiday together this last summer, and I suppose in a round about sort of way, Nette feels safe with Mum and Dad. But there is an emptiness now that Ian's gone from her physical life, but she can still find time to laugh, and has become so active socially, that Mum has to book an appointment to see her sometimes now!

The Wedding dandy and Dad 2002

All these people have been my friends at various stages of my life, and helped me and my family through very difficult times. I believe we would not have survived, as a family unit, had this not been the case. Their warmth and love has kept us going, and the fact that they <u>still</u> are my friends, amplifies this notion.

But, there is another group of people, that I have only talked about briefly, who have supported me during every breath I have taken. And they are my family. I did not choose them, and they certainly did not choose me, but together we have shared life's journey, and we are, mostly, still around to tell the tale.

I have two aunties, sisters of Dad, who have been to most of my big birthday parties over the years and sent me loads of stuff at Xmas and such like. Pam, best known for sending a birthday card a week early, or a week late, lives and teaches in Wolverhampton: she has a husband Greg, incidentally, the first person I ever smiled at, and two children, my cousins Claire and Paul, who make up her family. Claire and her husband Jonathan have two young children, Poppy and Isaac, and they all live with her long term partner, Jonathan. Paul lives with lovely Natalie in Telford, Shropshire. Then, over the Channel in Brittany, live Helen, a retired lecturer, Dad's wacky sister, and her husband John, a retired schoolteacher. Helen is the mother of my cousin Harvey. All my cousins are younger than me and hold really good jobs. But Dad's two sisters have been worth their weight in "wine", and have always been supportive for Mum and Dad on the phone, face to face, or on holiday or short break, even Brittany. Over the years they have offered advice to help with my development. Usually this has involved recommending either dietary needs or in understanding the need for supplements in my diet. The knowledge that they are just 'around' I know is a comfort to Mum and Dad.

My two aunties, and Dad, are the children of Doris and George Gordon, both of whom have, sadly, passed away. Nanny Gordon, Doris, spent a lot of time with me when I was young because she attended a course near my home so she could teach nurses as a clinical tutor, and she came to live with us for a while. She often played bowls and was good enough to be a county player. But what I enjoyed most about her was her orange VW car that I remember to this day, because when I see a similar Beetle Car I always turn my head and think, my Nanny Gordon had one of those. It was just like Mum and Dad's first car too. Gosh, the number of times me and Anna were shouted at in that thing: me for spilling food, and Anna for tweaking Dad's hair when he was driving. God, he used to go mad. Mum used to give him funny looks but he never took any notice. Nanny Gordon died a sad death, whilst quite young, in 1989 and I remember Dad and Mum going to her funeral.

Strange really in that Grandpops George was there at the funeral too. I say strange because when I was young I never saw much of him, because he didn't live with Nanny Gordon. They were divorced or something and I was about nine years old before I met him. Having lived in or near Derby for years, together with my Dad and his sisters, and then apart after their divorce, they didn't really seem to get on together. Much later in the 1990's Grandpops and Dad played golf together regularly, that was until Grandpops had difficulty walking because of leg ulcers. Shame, because he loved being physically active and one of his main hobbies was the Dunkirk Vets that he helped run as their Derby Branch Secretary. He really liked all soldier things and going with Dad, family and friends, over to France and Belgium regularly on pilgrimages, wearing his war medals proudly. Grandpops died this last year, March 2006, after a long illness, but Dad had just managed to get him over again to France, for one last time the previous June.

My mum's mum and dad were Ted and Peggy Starkings. Neither was called by their original names, which were Wilfred and Vera. This changing of names must be a country thing I think, because they were both brought up in the country before and after they met. They lived in Gorleston near Great Yarmouth. Granddad worked as a carpenter and we still have some of his work in our house to this day, despite my attempts to wreck them and most other things such as furniture. When Granddad died Nanny Peg stayed on her own in her house for eight years more, and now she lives with us for her health and safety. Mum and Dad were married in Gorleston in 1969, long before I was born. Following my birth many of my first holidays, away from Birmingham, were in Norfolk with Nanny and Granddad. Then we went on holidays to Devon with both of them. Since then I have been to Wales with Nanny, Devon with Dad, and Cumbria with Mum and Dad. Nanny Peg makes one of mine and Dad's favourite meals: beef pudding. This is an old recipe from

Buckinghamshire where Nanny hails from, and if I am totally honest and a snitch, my brother-in-law Mike, eats a whole one by himself! Nanny Peg used to work for Captain Birdseye in Yarmouth, and if she could have sold her 'beef pudding' recipe to him, I know she would be a millionairess today!

Me and Dad looking for ships in Gorleston

One other lady I've known all her life is my beautiful and charmingly funny sister Anna, who is so intelligent, that she has been all the way round the world. Really she has, she told me, and I've seen her photographs from all over the world to prove it. Anna has had such a charmed life ever since she was born, being my sister of course. For a start, she was born after Mum had a beef pudding for dinner the night before she was born on 18/09/1974. And, following a dash to the hospital in the early morning that she was born, the doctor gave Mum an epidural injection to help with the birth but it only froze her big toe! I couldn't stop rocking on my bottom with laughter when I heard this little gem being recalled by Dad on his return home from hospital that morning. He even sat with Nanny Peg drinking whisky at 7.30am in the morning, wetting my sister's head they said, before he went to teach. But I didn't smell any of the toast that they both seemingly talked about.

Anna at 13

Then when Anna and Mum came home Mum had to do lots more work with my new sister: feed her and change her smells, and lots more washing now there were two kids to look after. Though we had separate bedrooms, my little sister couldn't half scream. She kept me awake at night, and Mum too because she had to feed her. As she grew in size, and got older, Anna soon began to outstrip my own development crawling, walking and talking. All I could do was watch with envy, but at least I used to sit at the front of our double pushchair when Mum or Dad took us out!

I remember too that because I had problems, when Anna was two and a bit, she went to nursery for half a day, Monday-Friday, but that was while I was at school, so I didn't miss her. Sometimes, when Mum taught children in their own homes who could not go to school, Anna used to see Aunty Nette for an hour and Anna says she showed Aunty Nette how to colour in her books. Anna could read ever so well too and soon passed me at every other subject in school, and I was two years older than her! Not only that but she went dancing, and won medals, and kept on winning medals. That wasn't so bad because when Anna went to dancing school or competitions Mum took me in the car too. Sometimes I got to see Anna dance too, and one night, when she was ten years old she won the All England Junior tap dancing championship. And what was really amazing about that win was not only the hard work and effort she made, but that she had been diagnosed with insulin-based diabetes two years earlier. The condition never slowed her down though and in fact it spurred her into greater efforts. My sister was a district athlete, a swimmer as fast as any shark so dad reckons, just cos she can beat him I bet! And she was a dancer, an artist, good at school in lessons and a Duke of Edinburgh's Award winner. All those things I had wanted to do too, but never could. After taking her A-level examinations Anna went to university in Cardiff, and still kept on going out with the boyfriend she met at school, Michael, whom she later married.

They worked for two years in Birmingham and then went away for two years to Australia and most of the Far East and Europe. When they returned Michael went back into the police force and is now a senior policeman in Birmingham, and Anna now works for the Children's Society. On 6th November, 2006, I became an uncle. Anna gave birth to a beautiful baby girl, Ruby Grace. I know that my niece is developing well because I have seen, and heard her regularly! Having said that, I must say here and now, Anna has always been so good, kind and caring to me, as have all her friends down the years really. None of them ever ignored me. I get the same respect from those friends of Anna and Mike's as I do from Anna and Michael, and that makes me feel good inside. Anna really is one of my best friends ever, but not quite the best, because that must always be and always has been my Mum, Avril.

Anna 2000

My Mum and Dad.

I began saying that my Mum was my best pal, and how else could it be, or should it be? She bore me after a difficult pregnancy; she fed me; she noticed before anyone that I had a problem growing up; she has, with Dad, sorted out my education; she washes and irons for me without moaning, well sometimes; and she dresses me in really good kit that makes me look as normal as possible, even when I don't sound normal.

Andrew Give us a Kiss

In my first Suit that Mum bought for me

So who else could be my best friend, but my little Mum Avril? Mum grew up in Acle, then a small village in Norfolk, and after attending Acle Primary School and Great Yarmouth High School for Girls went to a women's PE College in Birmingham. Laid back, and so relaxed despite all the time she spends looking after me, she has also had to be alert for Dad's illnesses, and of course Anna's diabetes. Mum has saved dad's life twice and my sister Anna's life several times too. So now you see why it is so important to have someone around like my Mum, particularly when life is at stake, as I have just highlighted. And you should know that, despite all the problems that have entered her life since she married Dad, she not only copes admirably with all manner of situations, but incredibly is able, in conversation, to make the person she is speaking to feel like the most important person in the world. Good isn't she?!

I have been through many experiences with Mum and Dad, and but for Mum, I know, that I would not be here. I said Mum had saved Dad's life on two occasions, the first time being when he had encephalitis. The doctors kept telling Dad he had a cold or flu or something. However, when the fifth doctor came to our house Mum pinned him to the wall in the hall and said to him "Do not tell me again he has flu!!!!!!!!!!!!!!!!!!" Or words to that effect, so to speak. "Save my husband's life!!!!" An ambulance took dad to the then East Birmingham Hospital, and after a period of touch and go, he was to recover. Not before they told Mum to prepare for the worst. Later, they were to tell Mum that Dad was recovering but he might be wheelchair bound for life.

So whilst all that was going off with Dad, and she was trying to sort me out and my mess, no time for herself naturally, but Mum should have won the patience award for that year. Yes?

Ten months after his illness Dad was back playing football and cricket, and any other confounded ball game. Mum said he was a mad bugger or something, but he didn't stop there. Years later, during a performance of "Cats" at the Hippodrome, Dad had really bad chest pains that caused him to take a fast taxi home during the interval.

When Mum arrived home, after the show, Dad was dying at home in bed, or so the locum said. He called for an ambulance immediately telling Mum "He's a goner!" To say the least Mum was not happy I can tell you. Anyway, Dad was back in hospital again, survived, and is still with us happily moaning – Mum's words not mine! So, Mum saves Dad's life once more – is he lucky or what?

But, better by far was the day she saved Anna's life when my kid sister was only eight years old. Anna had been going through a bad time drinking lots of water and juices, and having problems with her wee. Mum said she thought Anna had a serious medical problem, and one Saturday afternoon with Nanny Gordon, instead of going for a walk in the park with me and Anna, turned right into Good Hope Hospital, Sutton Coldfield instead of left into the park. The A and E department was not ready for Mum who told the sister that Anna was ill, seriously ill, and suspected that the illness was diabetes. Poor nurse, she told Mum to take Anna to our GP for tests. Mum went into orbit and nearly took the nurse with her. The outcome, I hear you ask? Anna was admitted to the hospital there and then, and was in the hospital for three weeks as she adjusted to becoming diabetic.

Yet again Mum saved the life of a family member. You know she even diagnosed me as having a broken leg one day I came home from school. Seemingly some little girl at school had run into me with a trolley and snapped my tibia. Not wanting to be a wimp I never showed any concern, but I couldn't put my foot on the ground. Sadly, neither the school or taxi driver noticed my problem. Not so my Mum and because she was alert to my problem, whipped me into Good Hope Hospital where I was fast tracked into plaster up to my hip! She also spotted two lumps, one in each groin that turned out to be hernias. Following surgery, Mum stayed with me day and night till I was able to go home. A Mum in a million? You bet she is, and if anyone in my life deserves a cuddle, then it's her. Don't you agree?

My Dad's a good mate too. Since he had to pack up teaching he has taken me in hand and does everything for me, on the physical side, now that Mum is smaller than me. But really dad showers me, shaves me, cleans my teeth, dresses me and feeds me too. He cooks nearly all the meals we eat that include Indian and Chinese and all those spicy foods. He cuts up all my food, mashing it to a pulp before I eat it so as not to upset my digestion because I don't chew my food very well. But of course, I still wolf the food down. He drives me in his car, everywhere, driving me mad at times! We go along motorways, to airports, anywhere basically that there is noise because he thinks I like noisy things like trains and planes. Of course I do, but within limits, Dad. He took me to cricket matches, just me and him, and left me at the end of his bowling run up, over the boundary edge of course, so he could check me out! Sometimes his mate's kids would keep an eye on me, but I never let him down how could I? Anyway, I'm here to tell this tale.

Dad used to attend school near Derby: first the County Primary School, and then John Port Grammar School. Following A levels he went to college in Birmingham, took PE, just like Mum, which is the city where they met, and were to fall in love and eventually get married.

I've heard them both talk about the night they met, and the misunderstanding that followed. Apparently he scored six goals in a college soccer match in the afternoon, he says. And that same night, after dancing with Mum at a disco/dance or something our parents used to do, he was saying "cheerio" to Mum when another lady spoke to mum. It was, seemingly my mother's mother, and she was saying "cheerio" to her boyfriend! Dad didn't know Mum's mother had been at the disco, and thought it a bit weird that he had not been introduced to her. There lay the misunderstanding: it was Mum's "college mother", not her real mother. Oops!

From College Dad went to teach in North Warwickshire and then onto Chelmsley Wood (Solihull North) for thirty years until he retired through ill health. He still hasn't learned to relax even yet. It was after this illness that he gave Mum terrible problems as he tried to adjust to his free time. However, I love him to bits. I'm not well known for showing affection, but often I just <u>have</u> to put my arms around his neck and hug him. I stare long and hard into his eyes trying to convey my love for him, so I hope he understands this gesture.

So that's about it. I am so lucky to have the friends and family that I have, I feel I have been blessed, if not with ability, then with these lovely people who keep me going and look after me. But the future can only be as good as the past if I am able to continue having friends like these. We shall see.

Lessons we have all learned.

'Trial and terror' seems to have been the tenet for Mum and Dad coming to terms with, and learning to live with me, not only in the early stages but even today. Dad might have said, early in my life that they were urinating into the wind whilst trying to fathom out what had gone wrong with me in Mum's womb prior to my birth.

In the end I have tried to explain how my challenging behaviour, habits and idiosyncrasies can in some cases last all my life, but others can be temporary, even if they last for a few months or several years.

Lifetime examples of my habits still include my finger and thumb sucking that I found most comfortable and relaxing when I discovered how to do it, and my nose tapping that I have shown how to get others in trouble as my fingers split in shape to make a V-sign! These two, above all others, have always created more problems for other people than they have for me. But my wise old Mum always advises friends, and Dad, to ignore me, and when they do, guess what.....I nearly always stop the habit, temporarily.

Other mannerisms and routines I have described earlier so now I will, as I briefly indicated in the last paragraph, see what I and others in my circle have learnt from their experiences with me, and hopefully how we all grapple with some of our shared problems.

If I could make one observation from where I sit it would be that even after all the arguments, the tensions and shouting - and I mean Mum and Dad, at each other, not me this time - they are still together after more than 37 years of marriage. That, in itself, at least shows some form of loyalty to each other, and me, whatever testing times they have endured. Many of their acquaintances that have children with severe learning difficulties have split up, divorced, or lead separate lives rather than stay and work through their difficulties together. So praise where it's due to Mum and Dad. And when Dad learns to be as patient as Mum is with me, and there is still time left, then he will have learnt the biggest lesson of all: that it's no one's fault that I am like I am, and I have never meant to keep him, or Mum and Anna awake at night, or cause them undue stress. It is just nature, and, put simply, I am what I am. So Dad, start to chill out like Mum and enjoy life more.

Living with a child who has, amongst other medical complications, severe learning difficulties, has to be and often will be, a totally different and life changing experience for both parents and other family members. This has certainly been the case in my own family. My family has had to make sacrifices that are not usual in families that do not have members with disabilities. Their social life has been, decidedly truncated and may even change at the last minute. In my own case, I suppose as my development has maybe almost passed that expected of a ten month old baby, I have become more aware of how the family support each other and me, and this is crucial for our survival as a unit. This is also utterly true of my friends and carers. So too, in some cases, would be the support given by social workers, who my Dad says, have not been too proactive in their help and support, until of late.

However, that has changed recently, and Mum and Dad are much happier for the support given to us by a lady social worker called Bernie, and a community nurse, Lesley. This lady, who came to the house three times in one week to work for my future benefit, did what she said she would do! The same can be said for some nurses that have been involved with us, because their help and support has been continuous and consistent since my birth.

Changing tack completely, Dad always says he did his job better in teaching because of me. The way he and Mum related to the pupils not only because of their own skills, but they craftily on the odd occasion used me as the bait or blackmail in dealing with difficult children. How? Well as many of them already knew of my disabilities Dad used what he called functional blackmail to get his point across to the child. He would say to some naughty lad that he wished his son was as good as they were at sport or in lessons. And if he just picked the right moment, they would think about his comments, and maybe go away and try to improve themselves. I suppose that is manipulation by any other rule, but Dad says it was about motivation, or something called bullshit. But he says it often worked, so I suppose I had a purpose after all.

Another of the lessons learned concerns my passion sitting in cars and being driven around by Dad or anyone else. And one of my naughty ruses is to try and 'help' the driver on the journey by flicking the indicator stick to hear the noise the clicking indicators make; or holding the handbrake, and even changing gear sometimes especially when the car is idling at traffic lights. Catching the driver unawares gives me a thrill notably when I see the astonished look on their faces as they think, 'he didn't do that then, did he?' But now, when anyone new takes me out in a car, Dad always alerts them to my 'fun' and they look out for my hands moving towards the car's controls. On top of this, I have to sit in the back of a car now if I start to bounce around and use the seat as a trampoline. I just thought the seat was bouncy and had no idea I was being a hazard and danger to the driver. Still no great harm has come yet, to spoil a drive out in the country, and of course I have no intention of placing anyone, including myself, at risk.

I have often dwelt on my lack of development, or at least its slowness, but there have been times when I have striven and caught up normal children eventually. Eating at mealtimes, so long as the food is pulped or mashed, is one area where I think my manners are good, and I seldom leave the pattern on the plate to the delight of the cook! And let's not forget that most people have reactions to some foods, and my tummy sometimes rejects food too so that is quite normal as well. I have been known to eat all types of food from most continents: spicy, hot, fishy, fusion. However, Dad cheekily once gave me some of his chicken vindaloo one night, hoping I would disappear and leave him alone after he gave me a hot mouthful of curry. I amazed him because not only did I relish the spoonful of hot curry, but went back for more, putting his nose right out of joint.

Another positive skill I have acquired through 'trial and terror' is that of toileting. Mundane I know to most people, but when you have been in nappies of one sort or another until your late teens, the chance to have a dry bum and more freedom in one's "undies", is appreciated. Although I sit on the toilet at all times and do not stand, I can now take myself to the loo and perform naturally. There are occasions when I have an accident, of course, but Mum's patience in letting me get to the stage where I have become independent with my toileting, has paid off handsomely, for me at least.

However, I am told that since February 2005, my development has taken off by even greater leaps and bounds. Well, for me anyway. The trigger? Only a dose of Omega 3 fish oil taken daily, would you believe. For a young man with lots of autistic tendencies I now have new tricks in my repertoire that have stunned even the most sceptical of adults, at home with my family, or with staff at my day centre. These now include me eye-balling people, sometimes for quite some time. Not something I have ever done in the past, and not a trick that most of us autistic people perform usually. I actually cuddle other people now, of course only those I am familiar with, and never strangers, and don't mind people giving me a cuddle. This was something that in the past I did not tolerate at all because it wasn't macho enough, or that's what I think! How times change. I now laugh much more and there are many more smiles in my armour. In fact I am much more relaxed all round, and touch wood, I am sleeping longer which must be a relief to Mum and Dad. Even one of the ladies from ICS told Mum and Dad in my chat book that at times I can be "so loving" at times. Another skill that I have acquired involves my slippers of all things. Yes, Mum makes me change when I enter the house. She says to keep the carpets clean. But now when I get out of bed, or when I have been out of the house, I now look for my slippers usually under the telephone table, and when I find them place my feet into them carefully. Yes and they are always my own slippers, which for me is a giant leap forward, even if I get them on the wrong feet. All this leads me to think deep down that the comments folk make about my new progress are no longer a ploy to try and motivate me as such, but are in fact true.

This last paragraph leads me gently into what the future may hold for me, and essentially, where I will live in that future. I am told I shall have a normal lifespan, barring illness, and although Mum and Dad have begun to accept I will have to live away from them eventually, neither they, nor I, really want to face that day. There are homes around that have all the mod cons that cater, not only for persons like me, but also for the medical conditions I have. There are mattresses that can decipher the difference between a person rolling around in bed and when a person has a seizure. Or doors that open 180 degrees so someone can access a room at all times for safety. These homes are usually able to accommodate twenty to thirty clients and tend to be like small hospitals. But there are other homes that are smaller and develop more of a family atmosphere more easily than larger homes. And there are other homes that I know Mum and Dad will visit one day on my behalf. But really, I only have, or want, one home, and that's the home I've known all my life, with my Mum and Dad. So please God, help me to keep on improving my behaviour and leave all my disturbed behaviour in the bin of history, so that I can stay in my own home as long as possible. Please hear me God, your Andrew.

Andrew Give us a Kiss

ISBN 1425118151